Editor

Walter Kelly, M.A.

Managing Editor

Ina Massler Levin, M.A.

Cover Artist

Denise Bauer

Art Production Manager

Kevin Barnes

Imaging

Rosa C. See

Publisher

Mary D. Smith, M.S. Ed.

W9-AHL-651

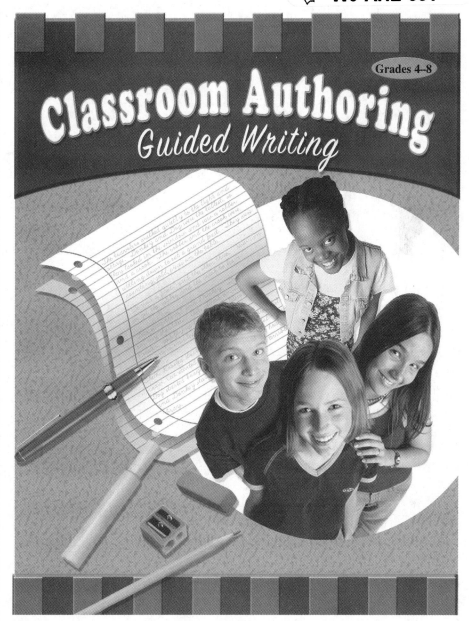

Grades 4–8

Classroom Authoring
Guided Writing

Author

Jima Dunigan, M.A.

Teacher Created Resources, Inc.

6421 Industry Way

Westminster, CA 92683

www.teachercreated.com

ISBN 13: 978-1-4206-3137-1

ISBN 10: 1-4206-3137-3

©2006 Teacher Created Resources, Inc.

Reprinted, 2006

Made in U.S.A.

Table of Contents

Table of Contents

Guiding Student Writers

Employing powerful techniques of guided instruction, this program replaces vague "writing experiences" with strong scaffolding needed for students to learn, master, and enjoy the craft of writing. The program is packed with specific help for the teacher and a rich supply of activities in vocabulary building, sentence writing, paragraph writing, journaling, essays, reports, and story writing. Following this program will result in your students becoming strong, confident, independent writers.

Types of Student Writers

Some students seem to have internal, intrinsic organizational and verbal skills. They are typically good readers who read frequently from a variety of genres. Other student writers always seem lost on that great white desert of notebook paper lying before them on the desk. They gather up little piles of misfit sentences here and inappropriate words there. They mishandle the tools of mechanics, spelling, and grammar. How do we get both groups of students on the same track?

Guided writing as a teaching method is effective for teaching writing to all ages, including adults. Most students can learn the methods used in this text and can transfer them to other writing assignments. In the classroom, it is effective to pair weaker writers with more capable students. The advanced writer can talk through the process while pulling ideas from the weaker writer. This scaffolding technique allows the weak writer time to acclimate to the planning, organizing, and writing process without draining the teacher's time. Most writers become self-sufficient after a period of scaffolding with a peer.

Modeling

It is important for the teacher to model an example of the type of writing assignment students will be expected to attempt. Students do not write during a teacher modeled example but may participate orally at the teacher's discretion. After modeling an entire sample of the assignment, you are ready to conduct a guided writing activity. Students need a guide to lead them through the first few attempts at a particular type of writing assignment.

Staying Involved

Stay involved in the entire process. Explain the assignment, explain the rubric or checklist, model a sample of the assignment, and then guide the class through each stage of the writing process. Keep all students on the same section (even the same sentence) at the same time. Pull feedback from random students. This allows classmates to hear examples of what is acceptable or appropriate. It also gives the teacher a valuable assessment of student progress.

Guiding Student Writers *(cont.)*

Re-Modeling

Sometimes it is necessary to model a type of writing assignment more than once. The teacher can gradually involve the students in writing their own papers. One method is to model the second example lesson while students copy the lesson during the process. Another method is to lead the students through a second modeled assignment, stopping at the last paragraph of the middle section. Because of the organization that took place during Plot and Plan, students will already know the item types to put into the paragraph.

Vocabulary and Research

Make vocabulary and information collection a vital part of every assignment. Early on, emphasize STAR vocabulary (see pages 20 and 22), information collection, and information organization.

Prompts

Teachers can supply prompts to the whole assignment, segments of the assignment, or even discrete sentences of the assignment. Teachers can require that specific information be included in a written work in a specific segment of the writing frame. Prompts help teachers support students through the guided method of writing.

Writing Frames

Writing frames provide external support and are an integral part of guided writing. Transitional writing frames supply transitional words and phrases in paragraph or essay format and leave blanks for the writer to complete. The writer refers back to a graphic organizer for the sequence and type of information needed for the blanks. After repeated use, students internalize the concepts and use them automatically. Thus, students mature in their thinking and begin creating writing structures to fit the writing occasion. Some writing frames have sentence or paragraph boxes that guide the students to sequentially supply specific information in a particular form of response. For example, in Prompt-Response Guided Paragraph Writing, one prompt guides the whole paragraph, and individual sentence prompts guide each sentence within the paragraph.

Feedback

During a lesson when students are writing their own papers, you need to hear from them. This feedback allows you to keep track of each student's grasp of the ideas as well as individual progress.

It is also important to give positive feedback to students as you hear their responses. Find ways to correct ideas while guiding students. For example, say, "That is one way, and I am thinking of another way. See what you think of this."

Timing

Do not allow students to go ahead of or lag behind the class during the crucial first few attempts to use a particular writing strategy. Teach the class to remain quiet while others finish a sentence or a section. Noise and distractions keep students off-task and slow the process.

Guiding Student Writers *(cont.)*

Timing *(cont.)*

Once instructions for a sentence or section are clear, tell the class how much time is left for that portion. Say, "You have 90 seconds to write the sentence responding to idea one on the sequence list." Students will soon understand that working quickly is important and that completing the task is a requirement. When time is up, ask, "Who needs 30 more seconds?" Teach students to respond silently by raising a hand and quickly getting back to work.

Withdrawing Support

As students gain independence in a strategy, give less and less support. *The goal of guided writing is for students to become independent writers.* Students can and will transfer writing skills learned in specific writing instruction class.

First Student-Teacher Conferences

After students develop a first draft, confer quickly with individuals and offer suggestions. With practice, teachers can hold 30- to 60-second conferences and may confer more than once with a student. Do not overwhelm a student with multiple directions. Instead, work on one or two tasks. You may need another conference after the first revisions. *Never assign a grade after the first draft.*

During the second draft writing, the teacher can begin a second round of conferences. If you used a simple frame for writing the first draft, it is easy to check for capitals, end marks, subjects and predicates, sentence variety, development of sub-topic sentences, supporting detail sentences, vocabulary, order of writing, or other rubric criteria. *The teacher and the student should use a writing checklist for editing.*

Assessment

After opportunities to revise, edit, and re-write, assess student writing for a grade. Use the same tool for assessment as for editing and revising, thereby guiding the student to mastery of assessment goals. Assessment of student work should be in a conference with the student present and participating for maximum value to reinforce basic good writing. Student involvement in evaluation promotes higher-order thinking.

Merging the Science and Art of Writing

Teachers (and eventually students) provide the science for writing in the form of graphic organizers, lists, frames, or charts. *Graphic organizers make thinking visible to the student and provide structure and order.* The student supplies the art of writing by selecting ideas, being creative with words, cultural language, prior knowledge, originality, and imagination.

Re-Teaching: Growth Takes Time

Several similar lessons appear in each section to develop mastery of a particular type of writing. Re-teaching allows students to internalize the skills and concepts of writing.

Guided Method of Process Writing

Step 1: Plot and Plan

- Understand the project
- Visualize the finished product
- Design graphic organizers
- Research information
- Develop STAR Vocabulary
- Organize materials

Step 2: Package the First Draft

Teachers guide students step by step, even sentence by sentence, through an assignment using graphic organizers, writing frames, or transitional frames. Teachers use timing strategies to help keep all class members on the same sentence or small section at the same time. When all students have completed that part, the teacher calls for feedback from students in the class. Students do not complete the first draft of an assignment alone until the process is mastered.

Step 3: Prune and Plump

(checklist for revising the first draft: student-teacher conference)

Structure

___ beginning, middle, ending

___ clear main idea

___ paragraphs present and correct

___ clear sequence and flow of ideas

Sentences

___ varied sentence beginnings

___ mixed simple, compound, and complex sentences

___ fluent and correct syntax

___ sentences say what was intended

___ I can improve each sentence.

___ I can complete unfinished details.

___ I can add more description.

___ I can correct obvious mistakes.

___ I can think about what others say.

Personality

___ conveys author's purpose

___ sets mood and tone

___ communicates with reader

___ is original and engaging

Step 4: Polish and Re-Write

(checklist for editing before final draft: student-teacher or peer conference)

STAR Vocabulary

Sensory

___ five senses   _____ movement

___ emotion

Technical

___ specific to the topic

Articulate

___ conveys clear meaning

___ fluent

___ transitional

___ free of redundancy

___ subject-verb agreement

___ correctly used words

Realistic

___ local vernacular

___ cultural dialect

___ appropriate phrases

___ true to characters and situations

English Standards

___ punctuation   _____ spelling

___ capitalization

Write a Final Draft

Step 5: Publish and Perform

- develop a portfolio
- post on a wall
- host a discussion
- print in newspaper
- keep a ring binder
- write in a book
- mail to a relative
- print in school news
- keep a folder
- read to family
- save in a capsule
- share among friends
- read aloud in class
- place in a scrapbook
- enter a contest

Golden Rules for Guided Writing

1. Know what you want from students—plan each step.

2. Model the writing process and activity.

3. Present examples and provide prompts.

4. Use graphic organizers.

5. Give instructions in specific, small bites.

6. Use rubrics for planning, writing, editing, and final assessment.

7. Guide students through each step of the process and stay involved.

8. Keep students on track: use timing to control progress.

9. Merge the science and the art of writing.

10. Require improvements in every draft.

11. Hold student-teacher and peer conferences.

12. Give positive feedback.

13. Celebrate success: display work, let students perform, share, reward.

14. Design a method of storage such as ring binders, folders, or portfolios.

15. Repeat the process. Growth takes time.

Guided Writing: Philosophies and Strategies

Guided Writing Incorporates Contemporary Philosophies of Learning

1. **Taxonomy of Learning** (from the works of Benjamin Bloom)
   - *knowledge*—remembering information
   - *comprehension*—understanding information
   - *application*—using a concept to solve a problem
   - *analysis*—breaking information into parts
   - *synthesis*—creating a new thing, combining different ideas
   - *evaluation*—judging the value of newly created materials or methods

2. **Multiple Intelligences** (from the works of Howard Gardner)
   - *verbal*—manipulate language for communication
   - *logical/mathematical*—manipulate numbers for purposes, use of logic
   - *spatial*—awareness of position and relationship of positions
   - *musical*—awareness of musical elements/manipulate sound
   - *bodily/kinesthetic*—ease and grace of movement/body control & awareness
   - *interpersonal*—keen perception of relationships between people/appropriate, wise intervention or response
   - *intra-personal*—honest, accurate knowledge of self
   - *naturalistic*—keen awareness of environment
   - *spiritual*—keen awareness of spiritual aspects
   - *technical/mechanical*—keen awareness of these relationships

3. **Experience in Education** (from the works of John Dewey)
   - Students must experience life and lessons to learn from them.
   - Best teaching practices actively involve students.

Guided Writing Incorporates Strategy Groups

1. **Research Activities**
   - *Brainstorming:* collecting what we know
   - *Conferencing:* conferencing before, during, and after writing
   - *References and Research:* using other sources to increase knowledge

2. **Writing Process Activities**
   - *Plotting and Planning:* brainstorming, organization, and planning
   - *Packaging First Draft:* first draft student-teacher conferences
   - *Pruning and Plumping:* revising and editing subsequent drafts
   - *Polishing and Final Draft:* final draft polishing
   - *Publishing and Performing:* publishing and presenting

Bloom's Taxonomy Applied to Writing

Writing presents a golden opportunity for teachers to lead students to higher-order thinking levels. In writing assignments, make sure to use terms and prompts from all of the taxonomy areas, especially analysis, synthesis, and evaluation—the three highest levels.

Lower to Higher Order Thinking

1. Knowledge

terms that demonstrate <u>knowledge</u> in writing:

list, record, match, cluster, label, name, recall, recount, sort, outline, define

2. Comprehension

terms that demonstrate <u>comprehension</u> in writing:

locate, identify, restate, paraphrase, tell, summarize, document, support, review, cite, explain, express, describe, recognize

3. Application

terms that demonstrate <u>application</u> in writing:

imagine, dramatize, apply, tell how to, show, imitate, organize, sequence, use, select, demonstrate

4. Analysis

terms that demonstrate <u>analysis</u> in writing:

break down, components, examine, map out, relate to, conclude, draw a conclusion, debate, defend, analyze, interpret, characterize, question, infer, distinguish, differentiate, classify, order, show similarities, show differences, compare to, contrast with

5. Synthesis

terms that demonstrate <u>synthesis</u> in writing:

compose, create, invent, construct, build, design, formulate, plan, synthesize

6. Evaluation

terms that demonstrate <u>evaluation</u> in writing:

compare, prioritize, evaluate, assess, argue, criticize, critique, predict, rate, judge, decide, categorize

Gardner's Theory of Multiple Intelligences Applied to Writing

Look in the nearby box. Howard Gardner's theory of intelligences says each person has a unique cluster of all of these types of intelligences. Each person has areas of greater and lesser strengths. The grape cluster below represents the whole person with his or her unique arrangement of talents. The whole picture helps define each person as a valuable individual.

Teachers and learners can use the idea of each person having his or her unique cluster of multiple intelligences to develop a positive sense of identity and to identify strengths. Each person's picture is equal to, but different from, everyone else's.

Using the "intelligences" words from the nearby box, write your greatest strengths on the larger grapes and your lesser strengths on the smaller grapes. You are someone special and unique. Tap into your strengths when you write essays, stories, reports, poetry, or letters.

- verbal
- logical/mathematical
- spatial
- musical
- bodily/kinesthetic
- interpersonal
- intra-personal
- naturalistic
- spiritual
- technical/mechanical

Self-Portrait: Each Person Is Unique and Valuable

A learner who is very social will write from a social-interpersonal perspective.

A learner who is strongly kinesthetic/bodily intelligent can imagine or act out movements and then write about them. Using innate strengths helps the learner to overcome and conquer weaknesses.

What Is Composition Writing?

Composition writing is expressive writing: collecting thoughts or information, ordering and refining thoughts or data, preserving thoughts or information on paper or electronically.

Writing causes deep-processing of information because the brain is actively involved in the process, as opposed to hearing or reading, which are more passive. Therefore, composition writing should be taught as an entity in its own right. *Writing integrates well with all subjects, but writing methods must be taught and all composition writing should follow a process.*

1. **Plot and Plan** (organizing and developing)

   Decide upon structure—shape, size, type, voice, audience, and scope of the composition. Collect and arrange data. Collect STAR vocabulary. STAR is an acronym for the types of vocabulary necessary in most writing assignments: (S)ensory, (T)echnical, (A)rticulate, and (R)ealistic.

2. **Package the First Draft**

   While developing the first draft, the writer chooses words, forms sentences, and uses the conventions of mechanics, spelling, and punctuation. The first draft is an attempt at firming up the thought process. The first draft may have weak or poorly formed sentences. It may be lacking in vivid diction (word choice). It may also have English convention errors in grammar and mechanics, spelling, or punctuation.

   Teachers should not judge or grade a written work at this stage. This is the time to hold teacher-student conferences. Writing frames like those found in this book allow mistakes and weaknesses to be easily spotted. Computer generated works on most word processing applications show some mistakes with red and green underlines. These are not foolproof, but they assist greatly.

3. **Prune and Plump** (revising the first draft)

   Using the frames, graphic organizers, and structures in this book greatly reduces the need for structural revision in writing. The writer may decide to add or remove supporting details, examples, reasons, or incidents, but the overall structure will remain intact. The next task is to improve sentences and sentence variety—e.g., mixtures of compound, complex, and simple sentences. The frames and other organizing structures in this book allow the writer to easily make small changes, even to a single sentence.

4. **Polish and Re-Write**

   Writers should do a final editing of the overall structure, sentences, vocabulary, and English standards. On a paper copy of a first draft, writer/editors can use colored markers or pens and do over-writes or use editing symbols. For a final draft, writers should strive for the highest standards of handwriting as well as English conventions. If the first draft is computer generated, the writer/editor can improve it by using various editing tools—insert, backspace, delete, spell, and grammar check. A teacher or peer editor can highlight areas for improvement. Before a final draft, there should be one last teacher-student conference or peer editing session. The final draft should be as nearly perfect as possible, observing English standards.

5. **Publish and Perform** (sharing the writing with others)

What Will Happen with Guided Writing?

1. **Students will learn that a single writing lesson using the guided writing process can and probably will take several class periods, even two or more weeks to complete a project.** The length of time required will vary depending upon the skill level and age of students, the size and scope of the assignment, and the allotted time for daily writing. Do not be alarmed and do not abandon the assignment. Guided writing is a systematic process guided by the teacher.

2. **Students will become independent writers as they internalize organizational patterns and writing process steps** during their guided writing experiences. Guided writing provides the external scaffolding and support for success while students learn to write.

3. **Students will begin to construct graphic organizers to fit their purposes** and will start to write independently. Students will transfer skills gained in guided writing lessons to all content areas.

4. **Students will accept, appreciate, and enjoy writing** as skill levels increase. Some students will become unexpectedly proficient and confident in writing.

5. **Some students will find their "voice" or identity** in writing.

6. **Even learning disabled students can achieve mastery** of the writing process and produce surprisingly high quality work.

7. **Some students may use writing as therapy** to express wounds, hurts, anger, intentions, and other emotions. Writing may lead the writer to identify and put into words those emotions that linger beneath the conscious level. Each student needs the opportunity to "journal" with some degree of privacy.

8. **Student writing scores will improve** dramatically.

9. **Some students will find vocations and careers in writing** because of the extra time and experiences provided by daily writing practice.

10. **Students will function on a higher level of thinking** while they are writing. If they are writing about a topic, their learning and memory retention for that specific topic will increase significantly.

Juggling Act

Writers bring personal learning style, background knowledge, cultural influences, different levels of skills, and preferences to the task of writing. Writers must juggle all of these as they plan, collect information, decide on a form, develop new ideas, put thoughts into words in unique ways, review what they have done, and produce a final draft. The diagram below clearly demonstrates high levels of brain activity during writing.

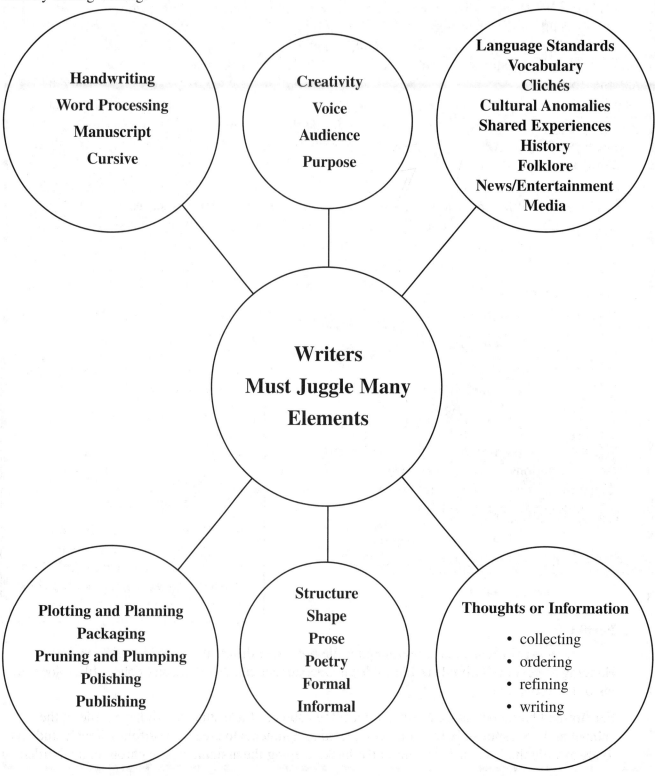

Classroom Management: Written Work

1. Ring Binders

Clear-view ring binders, sheet protectors, and floppy or CD disk holders help students manage their own work. Print names and class logos on colored paper and insert in the clear-view slots of the ring binders. Students pick up notebooks as they enter the classroom and put them away when they leave. Hole-punch each assignment sheet before handing it out and have students manage their own work thereafter, even over long periods of time.

Plastic sheet protectors

Three-ring binder   Disk holder   Front Cover and Spine Cover

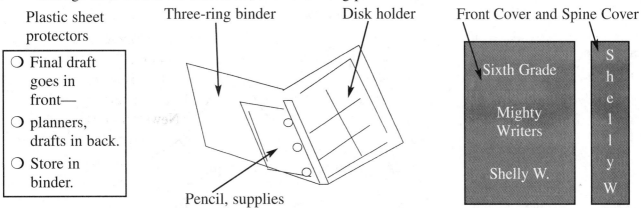

○ Final draft goes in front—

○ planners, drafts in back.

○ Store in binder.

Sixth Grade

Mighty Writers

Shelly W.

S h e l l y W

Pencil, supplies

2. Desktop Folders

Create a desktop folder for each student if possible. Students save drafts to the desktop and can also save drafts to the floppy or CD.

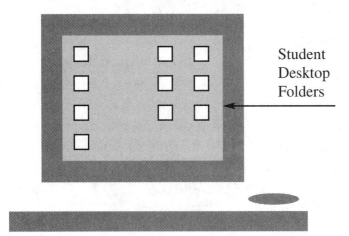

Student Desktop Folders

To create a student desktop folder on Windows:
- Right Click
- New
- Folder
- Backspace
- Type Student Name

Students start a new document in Word (or other word processing program) and then save to the folder. To open the folder later, double click the desktop icon and it will open.

3. Portfolios

For daily work, keep a small open-hanging file box. Use different-colored hanging folders. Hanging folders easily hold six file folders. One student can distribute and collect file folders in his or her group daily.

For finished hard copy assignments, use a filing cabinet. Each student will have a file in the cabinet and be responsible for filing completed assignments to create a portfolio. Teach students to always file the latest assignment in the back, keeping the assignments in chronological order.

Writing Ideas

Personal Experiences

something I heard
something I touched
something I smelled
something I tasted
something I saw
something I experienced
something that happened
a parent, grandparent, sibling, friend, or teacher
new friend
old friend
make-believe friend
neighbor
nurse
doctor
a gift I received

Letters

appreciation to teacher
appreciation to friend
to parent
to friend
to a company
to a political figure
to a relative
to a holiday figure
to a book character
to a company

Favorites

favorite color
favorite toy
favorite song
favorite holiday
favorite TV show
favorite place to go
favorite food
favorite flavor
favorite smell
favorite activity

Animals

pets: traits, training
animals that live in water
animals that live on land
animals that fly
animals that bite
animals that have fur
animals that lay eggs
animals in cold places
animals in the jungle
animals underground
animals that hunt
a flying animal
insects
spiders

Songs and Stories

words to a song
new song
poem
fairy tale
family story
community story
re-tell a library book
book reports
jokes
spin-off story
make-believe place
story about the city
story about the country
story about my nation
story about an argument
special event
story from an older relative
birthday party invitation
holiday card

Recipes

recipe a child can make
recipe for play-clay
holiday recipe
friendship recipe

Miscellaneous

commercials
advertisement
vacation
games and game boards
diaries
journals
grocery lists
newspapers
weather reports
news stories
schedules
charts
plays
instructions
certificates
rules
labels
observations
sentences
paragraphs
personal stories
responses

Student Written Books

book about a concept
book about numbers
book without words
book of information
alphabet book
predictable book
poetry
nursery rhymes
folktales
fables
drama
biographies
mysteries
retellings
environment book
biography

Revise and Edit Checklist

Prune and Plump

1. *Structure*
   ___ beginning, middle, ending
   ___ clear main idea
   ___ clear sequence and flow of ideas
   ___ strong supporting evidence and details
   ___ paragraphs present and correct, including dialog when present

2. *Sentences*
   ___ varied beginnings
   ___ mixed simple, compound, complex
   ___ writing says what is intended
   ___ complete details and description
   ___ no obvious mistakes

Polish and Re-Write

1. *STAR Vocabulary*
   Sensory
   ___ five senses
   ___ emotion
   ___ movement
   Technical
   ___specific to the topic
   Articulate
   ___ conveys clear meaning
   ___ fluent and correct syntax
   ___ transitional
   ___ free of redundancy
   ___ I can improve each sentence
   ___ subject-verb agreement
   ___ correctly used words
   Realistic
   ___ local vernacular
   ___ cultural dialect
   ___ appropriate phrases
   ___ true to characters

2. *English Standards*
   ___ punctuation
   ___ capitalization
   ___ spelling

3. *Personality*
   ___ communicates with the reader
   ___ original and engaging

Prune and Plump

1. *Structure*
   ___ beginning, middle, ending
   ___ clear main idea
   ___ clear sequence and flow of ideas
   ___ strong supporting evidence and details
   ___ paragraphs present and correct, including dialog when present

2. *Sentences*
   ___ varied beginnings
   ___ mixed simple, compound, complex
   ___ writing says what is intended
   ___ complete details and description
   ___ no obvious mistakes

Polish and Re-Write

1. *STAR Vocabulary*
   Sensory
   ___ five senses
   ___ emotion
   ___ movement
   Technical
   ___specific to the topic
   Articulate
   ___ conveys clear meaning
   ___ fluent and correct syntax
   ___ transitional
   ___ free of redundancy
   ___ I can improve each sentence
   ___ subject-verb agreement
   ___ correctly used words
   Realistic
   ___ local vernacular
   ___ cultural dialect
   ___ appropriate phrases
   ___ true to characters

2. *English Standards*
   ___ punctuation
   ___ capitalization
   ___ spelling

3. *Personality*
   ___ communicates with the reader
   ___ original and engaging

Assessment: Final Product Scoring Range

SCORE TALLY	DIMENSION	RANGE											
Maximum Score: 40	**Structure**	non-existent *				adequate *					superior *		
		0	1	2	3	4	5	6	7	8	9	10	
5 10 5 10 10	*Beginning, middle, ending *Clear main idea *Clear sequence and flow of ideas *Strong supporting evidence and details *Paragraphing present and correct												
Maximum Score: 15	**Sentencing**	non-existent *		adequate *			superior *						
		0	1	2	3	4	5						
5 5 5	*Varied beginnings, interesting *Simple, compound, & complex *Fluent and correct syntax												
Maximum Score: 20	**STAR Vocabulary**	non-existent *		adequate *			superior *						
		0	1	2	3	4	5						
5 5 5 5	*Sensory five senses, emotion, movement *Technical specific to topic *Articulate conveys meaning fluent transitional clearly expressed free of redundancy subject-verb agreement *Realistic local vernacular cultural dialect appropriate phrases true to characters and situations												
Maximum Score: 15	**Conventions of English Languate**	non-existent *		adequate *			superior *						
		0	1	2	3	4	5						
5 5 5	*Correct punctuation *Correct capitalization *Correct spelling												
Maximum Score: 10	**Personality**	non-existent *				adequate *					superior *		
		0	1	2	3	4	5	6	7	8	9	10	
Maximum Score: 100	**COMMENT:**												

Active Vocabulary Development

Students use vocabulary to organize learning and acquire or learn the meaning of words in order to increase learning. As a rule, therefore, vocabulary should be part of every organizational plan for writing. Vocabulary instruction and vocabulary collection as pre-writing strategies directly affect the quality of the writing product.

Vocabulary in the Content of Writing

Teaching vocabulary in content is highly effective. When students use vocabulary appropriate to the topic, they are operating in all areas of thinking according to Bloom's Taxonomy Applied to Writing. First, students recall or are taught vocabulary—*knowledge*. Students *comprehend* the vocabulary. Students then *apply* the vocabulary within their writing. Students *analyze* to examine, make conclusions, interpret, question, classify, compare, and contrast. Students *synthesize* when they use vocabulary to compose, create, invent, construct, design, and plan. Finally, students *evaluate* the vocabulary and the work they have constructed for correctness, effective and efficient use of words, and the overall product.

Essential Standard Writer's Vocabulary

Some words are essential to all writers. *Transitional vocabulary* assists organization and provides flow to written work. Teach transitional vocabulary to students as essential to all writing. Sensory words are also an essential word group. *Sensory words* give life and comprehension to writing. This chapter contains prepared lists of transitional and sensory vocabulary, leaving room for student additions. Distribute copies for student ring binders.

Content Specific Vocabulary

Collect and brainstorm content specific vocabulary as part of every writing assignment. Vocabulary can come from students, research, content materials, the culture, and other sources. Make a class vocabulary chart to post or have students make individual vocabulary lists as part of every writing assignment.

Once a content-specific vocabulary is created, it is a valuable product in itself. Type and print copies of class word lists for future use. Have students add these to the ring binders. Instruct students to keep vocabulary lists in plastic sheet protectors in front of the ring binders. Students will have easy access to content vocabulary during writing and for future reference.

Make Words Fun

Bring in age-appropriate poetry, jokes, puns, and riddles to share with students. Give students opportunities to share theirs. Ask how the words play on each other through *sound*, *definition*, *alliteration*, or *cultural association*. Encourage students to create poetry, jokes, puns, and riddles.

Some comic strips regularly play on words. Such strips, copied and duplicated or scanned and printed on a transparency, give the class a great opportunity to find humor with words.

Active Vocabulary Development (cont.)

Specific Lesson Guides

1. *STAR Vocabulary*

   Use a class period to teach the STAR Vocabulary concept. Hole-punch and distribute copies of STAR Vocabulary, found on page 22. STAR is an acronym for the types of vocabulary collection necessary for most writing assignments. The acronym STAR represents (S)ensory, (T)echnical, (A)rticulate, and (R)ealistic vocabulary words. Students will need a new copy of STAR Vocabulary for each writing assignment until creating STAR Vocabulary becomes automatic.

   Lead the class in developing a STAR vocabulary for a specific topic—e.g., "Dissecting Frogs in Science Class." Guide the students in brainstorming sensory, technical, articulate, and realistic words for the assignment. Demonstrate that STAR vocabulary lists can be made anywhere—on the board, an overhead transparency, blank sheets of paper, or poster boards. At first, students will need the STAR Vocabulary sheet on page 22. As students assimilate the idea of STAR vocabulary, they may no longer need the form but will create appropriate lists on their own.

2. *Fifty-Cent Words*

   Duplicate and distribute copies of the Fifty-Cent Words sheet on page 23. Have students add it to the vocabulary section of their ring binders.

   Recognize higher-order vocabulary in student speech. When a student uses a word that is surprising or pleasing, say, "That was a fifty-cent word; after the period, you get a reward."

   Write the student's name and the word on a sticky note and put it on the door or other designated "word spot." It will only take a few seconds. More students will make the effort to use higher order vocabulary in their speech. Higher-order vocabulary in speech is valuable, and it spills over into writing. The public recognition is more valuable to the student than the small prize you may give, but be certain to give the prize.

   Recognize higher-order vocabulary in student writing. Add a sticky note to the student's writing, and at an opportune time, read the sentence to the class, emphasizing the vocabulary word. Then put the sticky note with the word on the designated vocabulary spot. Find an opportunity for students to have a short session on adding words to the Fifty-Cent Word list in their ring binders.

3. *Word Posters*

   To call attention to sensory words, incorporate art into the writing class. See the Color Words Poster on page 24. Have students brainstorm color words and develop a color words poster. Then have them color those words appropriately. A 64-count box of crayons provides a great resource. Students can search catalogs and magazines for colors and cut them out in the shape of the word for the color. Students can paint their posters or use word processing tools on a computer and print out a color poster. Display the posters in class and encourage students to use those words in writing. Students are more likely to use color sensory words after this activity.

Active Vocabulary Development *(cont.)*

3. *Word Posters (cont.)*

   Similar procedures may be used for these other word poster suggestions:

   - Appearance Words
   - Fast Movement Words
   - Sounds Words
   - Touch Words
   - Emotions Words

   - Time Order Words
   - Spatial Order Words
   - Degree Words
   - Compare and Contrast Words
   - Friendship Words

4. *Writer's Essential Vocabulary*

   Hole-punch the Writer's Essential Vocabulary: Sensory Words on pages 27 and 28 and distribute copies to the class. Lead a class discussion and discovery lesson on sensory words.

   Hole-punch copies of the Writer's Essential Vocabulary: Transitional Words on page 29 and distribute to the class. Lead a class discussion on how to use transitional words to give flow and order to writing.

   Hole-punch and distribute the two-page lesson titled Writer's Essential Vocabulary: Prepositions on page 30.

   Lead the class in an examination of the preposition list. Students will see unfamiliar words. Assign different students to find definitions. Guide students through the second page explanation of prepositions and lesson activities.

   Students can store the copies in plastic sleeves in ring binders or some other management system best for your classroom. Students should have the vocabulary sheets available to them as they write during the year. Encourage students to use a variety of sensory words and transitional words in their writing and to vary choices for different assignments.

5. *Good Literature: Read Aloud and Read Often*

   Read often from a wide variety of quality literature, even to eighth graders. Children's trade books have real and relevant literary value to all people. Discuss vivid word choice in those books. Ask, "What word choices make the story come alive?" Bring in vivid quotations from a variety of sources, such as novels, newspapers, and magazines. Examine figurative language in those selections.

6. *Teach Discrete Skills—Directly and Imbedded*

   As a writing teacher, you will begin to identify frequently occurring words and word usage errors such as subject-verb agreement, misuse of apostrophe, tense, spelling patterns, and wordiness. Find or create specific lessons that focus on development of that vocabulary skill. Demonstrate the correct use of the skill and have students practice and apply the skill.

Teach specific word skills and active vocabulary development. If you want it, teach it!

STAR Vocabulary

Name _____   Date _____

Assignment Title _____

Sensory	Technical	Articulate	Realistic
List five senses words: *touch*, *taste*, *smell*, *hearing*, and *sight*. Add *emotion* or *feeling* words and *movement* or *motion* words.	List *technical* and *jargon words* and *phrases* specific to the topic of the assignment, report, essay, or story	List words and phrases that *convey intended meaning*. The words are fluent and clearly expressed; *include transitional words*, *adjectives*, and *adverbs*	List local *vernacular*, *cultural*, *dialectal words and phrases* appropriate to the story, characters, or situation.
_____	_____	_____	_____
_____	_____	_____	_____
_____	_____	_____	_____
_____	_____	_____	_____
_____	_____	_____	_____
_____	_____	_____	_____
_____	_____	_____	_____
_____	_____	_____	_____
_____	_____	_____	_____
_____	_____	_____	_____
_____	_____	_____	_____
_____	_____	_____	_____
_____	_____	_____	_____
_____	_____	_____	_____
_____	_____	_____	_____
_____	_____	_____	_____
_____	_____	_____	_____

Fifty-Cent Words

Name _____   Date _____

Word   **Short Definition**

_____   _____

_____   _____

_____   _____

_____   _____

_____   _____

_____   _____

_____   _____

_____   _____

_____   _____

_____   _____

_____   _____

_____   _____

_____   _____

_____   _____

_____   _____

_____   _____

_____   _____

_____   _____

_____   _____

Color Words Poster

red	purple	yellow
green	orange	aqua
black	white	silver
teal	maroon	cardinal
gold	crimson	wisteria
burgandy	lime	blue
olive	turquoise	navy
beige	milky	emerald
pearl	ivory	flesh
light	fuchsia	dark

A Word About Word Posters

- Making word posters is appropriate for many writing activities. When students make their own word posters or word lists, they tend to have more ownership and command of the words, use the words more frequently in writing, and remember how to spell the words.
- Assign students to use a word processing program and a word resource, such as a thesaurus, to create a poster of colors.
- Students can draw bubble letters to spell color words and fill them with the appropriate color crayon. (A crayon box is a good source of color words.)

Activities

- Choose a word and write a poem about the word.
- Write an acrostic poem using a color word.
- Choose a color to identify your personality and write a poem, paragraph, or essay.

Appearance Words Poster

slender

glistening

swollen

graceful

lumpy

dull

chubby

crooked

shadowy

cluttered

glowing

shabby

muscular

muddy

steep

freckled

Fast Movement Words Poster

scampered

bounce

darted

pounce

SHOOT

spring

SHOT

sprang

raced

Propelled

Rocketed

sprung

Sped

ejected

Galloped

streaked

Writer's Essential Vocabulary

Sensory Words

Writers use sensory vocabulary to convey sight, sound, smell, touch, and taste to the reader's sense of imagination. Sensory vocabulary brings writing to life. Use sensory vocabulary words from the lists below in your writing. Add to the list.

← — Sight Vocabulary — →   ← — Sound Vocabulary — →

APPEARANCE	COLOR	MOVEMENT	Loud Sounds	Soft Sounds	Vocal Sounds
bent	aqua	amble	crash	sigh	puff
bowed	azure	crawl	thud	murmur	scratch
chubby	beige	creep	roar	whisper	chink
circular	black	dive	screech	whir	stutter
cluttered	blue	dart	whistle	rustle	stammer
crooked	brass	dash	whine	twitter	giggle
curved	bronze	drift	squawk	patter	whimper
domed	cardinal	drive	blare	hum	coo
dull	creamy	flap	rumble	hiss	chatter
dumpy	crimson	flick	grate	peep	growl
flat	dark	flip	slam	buzz	snort
frazzled	dusky	flop	jangle	gurgle	whistle
freckled	emerald	gallop	clash	swish	whisper
fresh	fuchsia	hurl	racket	chime	whine
gigantic	gold	jab	thunderous	tinkle	raspy
glistening	green	jerk	deafening	clink	titter
graceful	heather	lap	piercing		chuckle
hard	ivory	lunge	squall		snigger
humped	jade	map out	throb		snicker
jagged	light	move	thump		simper
lumpy	lime	nod	bang		smirk
messy	magenta	nurture	knock		teehee
muddy	maroon	rip	smack		soft laugh
nasty	mauve	saunter	whack		guffaw
natural	milky	slink	thwack		horse laugh
oval	navy	spring	clip		roar
rectangular	olive	stalk	swat		cluck
regal	pearl	streak	rap		throaty
shabby	purple	swoop	rumbling		
shadowy	rainbow	trip	boom		
square	red	trot	crack		
squiggly	silver	twirl	echo		
striped	steel gray	twaddle	peal		
swollen	teal	wade			
tattered	turquoise	yawn			
triangular	wisteria	zip			
wavy	yellow	zoom			

Writer's Essential Vocabulary *(cont.)*

Sensory Words *(cont.)*

← ——— Touch–Taste–Smell ——— → ← ——— Emotional Words ——— →

Touch Words	Taste Words	Smell Words	Anger	Love	Fear
slimy	sweet	sweet	rage	ardor	dread
dusty	salty	perfumed	furious	adoration	fright
steamy	bitter	sharp	steamed	devotion	foreboding
slippery	sour	musty	burnt up	fondness	terror
spongy	tart	fumes	boil	tenderness	panic
mushy	briny	reek	flamed up	amity	threat
waxy	spoiled	stink	enraged	esteem	horror
rubbery	rotten	stench	flare up	infatuation	affright
leathery	buttery	odor	fly off	amour	apprehension
silky	smoky	malodorous	irascible	affection	alarm
velvety	burnt	wisteria	maddened	regard	dismay
wooly	vinegary	rose	wrathful	attachment	trepidation
prickly	fruity	cinnamon	fuming	emotion	consternation
gritty	tangy	fetid	violent	esteem	disquietude
fuzzy	medicinal	fresh-smelling	vehement	affinity	quaking
oily	fishy	onion	intense	compatibility	qualm
furry	peppery	meaty	fierce	congeniality	anxiety
hard	spicy	apple	provoked	cordiality	worry
soft	nutty	cheesy	rabid	charity	concern
jelly like	savory	coffee	wild	good will	fearfulness
brittle	tangy	unpleasant	fanatical	benevolence	cowardice
fragile	smack	pleasant	unbalanced	solicitude	phobia
slick	piquancy	fragrance	tumultuous	strong liking	nightmare
coarse	weak	bouquet	rampant	predilection	concern
bumpy	flat	emanation	savage	penchant	awe
rocky	common	fetor	passionate	partiality	wonder
calloused	luscious	aroma	unrestrained	inclination	veneration
hardened	toothsome	scent	reckless	beloved	ominous
flexible	scrumptious	garlic	heedless	relish	tremulous
tender	flavorsome		wild		nervous
frigid	spicy		fury		skittish
cold	appetizing		lunacy		scared
warm	hot		insanity		chickenhearted
chilled	zestful		agitation		timid
wet					diffident
icy					

Writer's Essential Vocabulary

Transitional Words

Time Order	Spatial Order	Degree	Comparison	Contrast	Cause and Effect
first	in front	more	similarly	however	since
last	behind	most	as	instead of	thus
later	next to	good	like	by contrast	due to
afterwards	nearest	better	likewise	nevertheless	as a result
second	farthest	best	neither/nor	yet	because
third	above	pretty	either/or	opposed to	consequently
soon	on the right	prettier	in addition	but	owing to
meanwhile	on the left	prettiest	outside	unlike	accordingly
always	in the middle	mainly	than	contrary	therefore
before	below	third	by comparison	nonetheless	for this reason
eventually	outside	least	more		so
then	inside	least significant	less		if/then
finally	nearest	most significant	better		
next week	under	weak			
tomorrow	underneath	weaker			
next	lowest	weakest			
earlier	highest	less important			
in the future	middle	first			
after this		equally important			
		second			
		most significant			

Writer's Essential Vocabulary *(cont.)*

Prepositions

Prepositions show time, space, movement contrast, or comparison relationships between two objects or elements. Words often used as prepositions appear on this page.

a la	as regards	in between	saving
abaft	as to	inclusive of	since
aboard	astraddle	in memoriam	subsequent to
above	astride	inside	than
absent	as well as	inside of	the
about	at	instead of	thorough
according to	athwart	into	through
across	atop	irrespective of	throughout
afore	back of	less	till
afoul of	bar	like	times
after	barring	mid	to
against	bating	midst	touching
ahead of	concerning	minus	toward
aloft	considering	near	towards
along	contra	nevertheless	under
alongside	contrary to	next	underneath
alongside of	cross	next to	unless
amid	despite	nigh	unlike
amidst	down	notwithstanding	until
among	due to	past	unto
anent	during	pending	up
anti	ere	per	up and down
apart from	except	plus	up to
après	except for	preparatory to	upon
apropos	exclusive of	previous to	upside
apropos of	failing	prior to	versus
around	following	pursuant to	_____
as	for	qua	_____
as far as	fore	regarding	_____
as far	forth	regardless of	_____
aside	forth of	relative to	_____
aside from	fro	respecting	_____
aslant	from	round	_____
as of	in	sans	_____
as per		save	_____

Writer's Essential Vocabulary *(cont.)*

More About Prepositions

Prepositions show relationships between words.

Prepositions usually come before <u>nouns</u> or <u>pronouns</u>.

Prepositions can show *place* relationship.

article	*subject noun*	*verb*	*preposition*	*article*	*object of the preposition noun*
The	cat	was	<u>below</u>	the	tree.

<u>Cat</u> and <u>tree</u> are two nouns that have a relationship. The cat was <u>below</u> the tree.

Place relationship prepositions include:

above	upon	within	in	out	into
by	across	from	toward	under	outside
beyond	behind	along	among	inside of	up
down	on	below	beneath	around	over
rear	through	onto	beside	between	at
past	to	in between	inside		

Prepositions can show <u>time relationship</u>.

subject noun	*verb*		*preposition*	*object of the preposition noun*
Sherri	came	home	after	six o'clock.

Time relationship prepositions include:

after	during	while	when	afterwards
meanwhile	till	until	before	

- **In English language sentences, place usually comes before time.**

- **A prepositional phrase is the preposition and its object.**

- **A preposition must have an object; therefore a preposition generally will not be found at the end of a sentence.**

Example prepositional phrases:

in the library	at the movies	in Europe	in the house
beyond the fence	below the wall	behind the tree	beneath the bed
out of the box	towards the sun		

Teaching Sentences

If You Want It, Model It!

Model the type of sentence you want, and you will get it back!

Start Simple

Even some fourth through eighth grade students need to learn to write simple sentences. Begin teaching simple sentences with the "subject, predicate, stop" approach. Re-phrase that to "*Who* (person, place, thing, or animal) *did what* (action or being-existence)."

Sentence Variety

- Teach students to identify a run-on sentence.
- Teach the use of the colon and semicolon.
- Teach three types of sentences: simple, compound, and complex.
- Teach students to vary sentence beginnings.
- Teach students to enrich sentences with description.

Connect with Conjunctions

- Re-teach conjunctions—*and, or, nor, for, but—to connect two simple sentences.*
- Teach coordinating conjunctions as "buddy" conjunctions—*both sides are independent.*
- Teach subordinating conjunctions as "bossy" conjunctions—*one clause is dominant.*
- Teach "clause" as being equal to a simple sentence—*having a subject and predicate.*
- Teach "phrase" as a group of words *missing a verb or noun or both.*
- Teach semicolon to *join two related simple sentences in the place of a conjunction.*

Robin Hood to the Rescue

Distribute "golden" adjectives and adverbs and their helpers among poor simple sentences. Make and display adjective and adverb posters in the classroom.

Guided Sentence Building

Make transparency copies of the Guided Sentence Building sheets on the next two pages. Use them on the overhead projector and demonstrate the skill of writing rich sentences. Start on the first line with a single-word subject and a single-word verb. On the second line, tell more about the subject and more about the verb. Again, on the third line write more information about the subject and the verb. Guided Sentence Building for compound and complex sentences appear farther along in this chapter on pages 45–53.

Practice Sentence Patterns

Duplicate and use the practice activities on pages 44–48 to provide students with practice in writing and punctuating sentences using varied sentence patterns.

Name _____

Date _____

Guided Sentence Building 1

Subject	Predicate
(Start with a capital letter.) (person, place, thing, or animal)	(action or being) (End with .?!)
_____ _____	_____ _____
_____ _____	_____ _____
_____ _____	_____ _____

Name _____

Date _____

Guided Sentence Building 2

Subject

Predicate

Name_____   Date_____

Building Sentences
with a Sentence Wheel

Write a variety of sentence endings on the outer segments of the wheel below. Write sentences that tell *who*, *what*, *when*, *where*, *why*, and *how*.

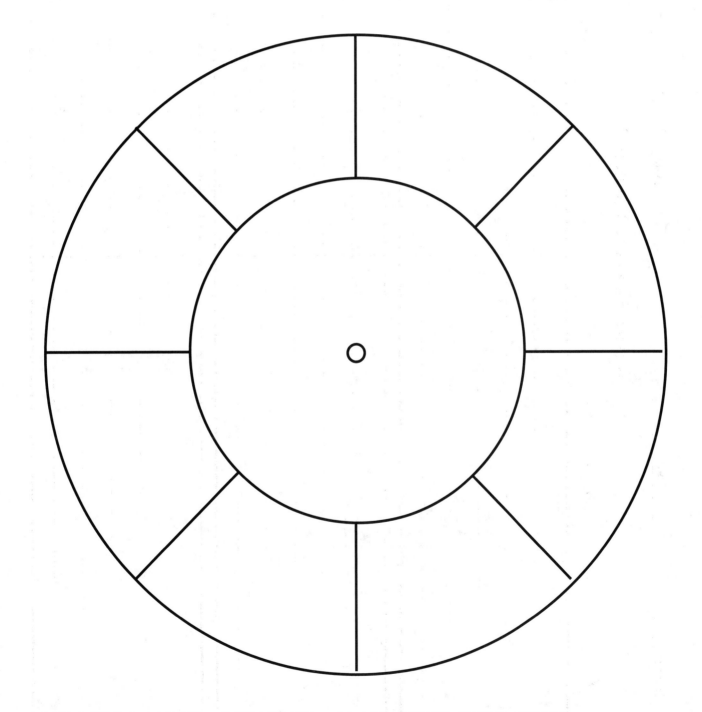

Name_____ Date_____

Building Sentences with a Sentence Wheel *(cont.)*

Write sentence subjects on the small sentence wheels on this page. Then, cut out the circles and attach them with a paper fastener to the top of the small circle on the previous page. Rotate the circles to make interesting (and perhaps unusual) sentences. Start each sentence beginning with a capital letter. Have fun.

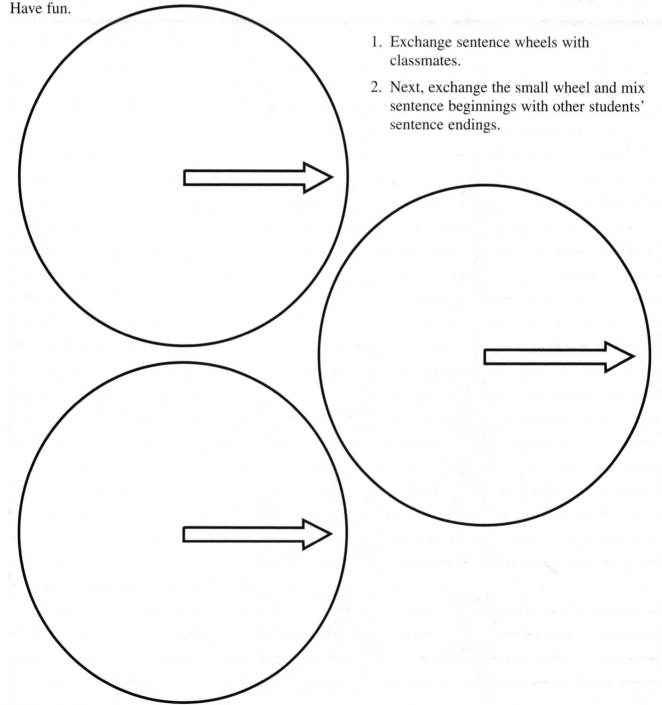

1. Exchange sentence wheels with classmates.

2. Next, exchange the small wheel and mix sentence beginnings with other students' sentence endings.

Name_____ Date_____

Building Sentences—
Practice Makes Perfect

Article	Noun		Verb
Choose a beginning for each sentence.	Choose a singular or plural noun.		Create a verb list. Choose a correct verb to match the noun. The verb you choose helps the reader know the time of the sentence, also called the *tense*.
A, An, The	cat	cats	dances, danced, is dancing
Some	dog	dogs	
Two	boy	boys	
Three	girl	girls	
	man	men	
	woman	women	
	chair	chairs	
	ring	rings	
	rock	rocks	
	bridge	bridges	
	elephant	elephants	
	goat	goats	
	frog	frogs	
	soccer ball	soccer balls	
	orange	oranges	
	pickle	pickles	
	train	trains	
	ostrich	ostriches	
	dinosaur	dinosaurs	
	go-cart	go-carts	
	fungus	fungi	
	printer	printers	
	monitor	monitors	
	telephone	telephones	
	lightning	lightning	
	rain	rain	
	deer	deer	

Building Sentences— Compound Subjects

A re-telling of "The Bremen Town Musicians" (original story by the Brothers Grimm)

Teaching the Lesson

Skills: subject/predicate patterns and compound subject/simple predicate patterns.

Materials: student copies of the story, compound subject sentence frames, transparency copy of the lesson, fine point markers, overhead projector

Performance Outcome: Students will re-write the story "Bremen Town Musicians," using sentences with compound subjects.

Teach Step 1

Using an overhead projector, marker board, or chart paper, you will demonstrate sentences that have compound subjects.

First, remind students that a sentence must have a *subject* and a *predicate*.

- Subjects tell the **"who"** of the sentence. Subjects may be any noun (person, place, thing, or animal).
- Predicates tell **what happens** or happened in the sentence.

A boy / skated on the sidewalk.

- "A boy" is the *subject;* "skated on the sidewalk" is the *predicate.*

A duck / paddled in the pond.

- "A duck" is the *subject;* "paddled in the pond" is the *predicate.*

Explain to students that sentences can come in many sentence patterns. The sentences above are simple sentences with one subject and one predicate. Sentences can have more than one subject with only one predicate.

Steven and Jason skated on the sidewalk.

- "Steven and Jason" is a *compound subject.*

A duck and a goose paddled in the pond.

- "A duck and a goose" is a *compound subject.*

Solicit several simple sentences with simple subjects and write them on the board. Ask students how they can make compound subjects from simple subjects.

Teach Step 2

Tell students that you are going to read an old story, "The Bremen Town Musicians." After the story, you will lead them to re-write the story.

Building Sentences— Compound Subjects (cont.)

Bremen Town Musicians

(Original Story by the Brothers Grimm—Re-telling by Jima Dunigan)

Once, long ago there was an old donkey. He worked very hard for his master for many years. The master thought the donkey was too old to be of benefit, so he decided to get rid of him. The donkey heard about the master's plans and ran away instead. He decided to go to Bremen Town and become a musician.

Down the road just a short distance, he met a dog. The dog was tired. Donkey asked Dog why he was so tired.

Dog said, "My master does not want me any longer, so I have decided to run away."

Donkey said, "Join me, I am running away, too."

Donkey and Dog met a cat. The cat was sad and crying a cat's cry about how unloved she was. Her master did not want an old cat that did not hunt mice.

Donkey and Dog invited Cat to join them.

Just a little farther down the road, Donkey, Dog, and Cat heard a mournful crowing sound in the middle of the day. They came to a farm and saw a rooster.

"Why are you crowing in the middle of the day?" they asked.

"I am old and the lady of the house does not need me anymore. She is planning to make chicken and dumplings come Sunday."

"Come with us to Bremen," the three travelers pleaded. "We will sing and be musicians in Bremen."

"Yes, I will," said Rooster.

That night, the tired, hungry travelers stopped near a forest. Donkey lay down under a big old tree to sleep. Dog lay down on the other side of the tree. Cat climbed to a high branch and settled in to rest. Rooster flew to the top, top branch. When it got fully dark, Cat started meowing. The meowing woke the others.

"I see a light deep in the forest," said Cat.

"Let's go see if there is any food," said Rooster.

Building Sentences— Compound Subjects (cont.)

Bremen Town Musicians (cont.)

The travelers walked quietly to the light and found a cottage. Donkey and Dog were the tallest, so they looked in the window and saw a robber and a crook. The robber and the crook were settling down to eat a grand feast. They were counting gold pieces on the table.

"We need a feast," said the others. "How can we get the robber and the crook to leave?"

"Let's scare them," said Donkey. "Dog, climb up on my shoulders. Cat, climb on Dog's shoulders. Rooster, you fly up to Cat's shoulders. When everyone is in place, start singing."

Then, Rooster started crowing his most dreadful crow, Cat started meowing her most awful meow, Dog started baying his most mournful howl, and Donkey started braying his most terrible bray.

Robber and Crook looked at the horrible monster in the window. At once, they went crashing out the door and ran away into the woods. They thought a goblin was after them.

The four friends sat down and ate a belly full of feast. Then they felt sleepy. Dog and Cat found comfortable places to sleep on the floor of the cottage. Rooster and Donkey went outside to sleep.

Later, Robber and Crook came back to see what had scared them. Just as they were looking into the window, Rooster flew down from the branch and started scratching and crowing. Donkey woke up and started braying and kicking. Dog sprang out the door and started baying and biting. Cat jumped upon them and started scratching, spitting, hissing, and yowling.

The robber and the crook ran away again and never did return to the cottage. Everywhere they went, they told of the great goblin with many arms and legs, some with claws and some with hooves, that took their cottage in the forest.

Any time after that, if a traveler was traveling near the woods on a warm summer night, he might have heard the musicians making their music. As time went on, many tales circulated about the terrible noise from the Great Goblin that lived in the woods. Donkey, Dog, Cat, and Rooster lived happily and safely in their cottage for the rest of their lives.

Building Sentences— Compound Subjects *(cont.)*

Teach Step 3

You may opt to read the story more than once, discussing the elements of the story:

Characters   Setting   Problem   Solution

Teach Step 4

Distribute copies of the student lesson on pages 42 and 43. Read instructions to students.

Directions: Create compound subjects for the predicates provided on your lesson sheets. Join compound subjects in this activity with the conjunction *"and."*

The Rule: Sentences may have compound subjects. Sentences with compound subjects have more than one simple subject but may have only one predicate.

Tell students that the work page is divided into two columns. In the first column, students will write the two subjects of the sentence. Students should follow the story line to create answers.

Usually accepted answers:

1. First, Donkey and Dog joined together to go to Bremen.
2. Then, Cat and Rooster joined donkey and dog to go to Bremen.
3. That night, Donkey and Dog made themselves comfortable under a tree.
4. Cat and Rooster went high into the branches of the tree to sleep.
5. Rooster and Cat looked into the distance and saw a bright light shining in the night.
6. Donkey and his friends followed the bright light to a cottage.
7. Donkey and Dog were the tallest so they looked in the window.
8. Crook and Robber were sitting at a table eating a feast and counting their gold.
9. Cat and Rooster stood on the backs of Donkey and Dog and they all began making their music.
10. Cat and Rooster crowed and meowed.
11. Donkey and Dog brayed and howled.
12. Crook and Robber thought a goblin was after them, so they ran away.
13. Then, Donkey and his friends sat down to eat the feast. Soon they were full and sleepy.
14. Dog and Cat found sleeping places in the cottage.
15. Donkey and Rooster found sleeping places outside.
16. Crook and Robber returned, but the four friends frightened them away again.
17. Donkey and his friends lived happily in the cottage and never did go to Bremen.

Teach Step 5

- Have each student write and illustrate a book, or each student write one page to be assembled into a class book.
- Have students re-write one sentence in the bottom box of each page and create the appropriate illustrations. Students should put page numbers on the book.
- Have students make and illustrate front covers for the books
- Have students bind the books by stapling or other means.
- Have students publish and share the books.

Name_____ Date_____

Building Sentences— Compound Subjects *(cont.)*

Read or listen to the story "The Bremen Town Musicians" by the Brothers Grimm.

In this exercise, write compound subjects with one predicate.

Directions: Finish the sentences below by creating compound subjects for the predicates on the right. Join compound subjects in this activity with the conjunction *and*.

	Create Compound Subjects		Predicates
1.	First,	*and*	joined together to go to Bremen.
2.	Then,	*and*	joined Donkey and Dog to go to Bremen.
3.	That night,	*and*	made themselves comfortable under a tree.
4.		*and*	went high into the branches of the tree to sleep.
5.		*and*	looked into the distance and saw a bright light shining in the night.
6.		*and*	followed the bright light to a cottage.
7.		*and*	looked in the window.
8.		*and*	were sitting at a table eating.
9.		*and*	stood on the backs of Donkey and Dog and they all began making their music.
10.		*and*	crowed and meowed.
11.		*and*	howled and brayed.
12.		*and*	thought a goblin was after them.
13.	Then,	*and his*	sat down to eat the feast.
14.		*and*	found sleeping places on the floor of the cottage.
15.		*and*	found sleeping places outside.
16.		*and*	returned.
17.	*From that time on,* Donkey and his _____		lived happily in the cottage and never did go to Bremen.

42

Building Sentences— Compound Subjects *(cont.)*

Illustration(s)

Write a short paragraph about something you learned from the story. Use compound subjects.

Sentence Patterns

1. Simple Sentences

<u>**Sara**</u>   <u>**practiced** the trombone.</u>
subject   predicate

_____
subject   predicate

_____
subject   predicate

_____
subject   predicate

<u>**Sara and Karen**</u>   <u>**practiced** the trombone.</u>
compound subject   predicate

_____
compound subject   predicate

_____
compound subject   predicate

_____
compound subject   predicate

<u>**Sara and Karen**</u>   <u>**practiced and played** the trombone.</u>
compound subject   compound predicate

_____
compound subject   compound predicate

_____
compound subject   compound predicate

_____
compound subject   compound predicate

Sentence Patterns *(cont.)*

2. Compound Sentences

Connect two simple sentences with a comma plus a conjunction to make a compound sentence.

Sara	practiced the trombone	,	and	Karen	practiced the violin.
subject	predicate	comma	conjunction	subject	predicate

conjunctions		
but		or
for	and	so
nor		yet

subject	predicate	comma	conjunction	subject	predicate

subject	predicate	comma	conjunction	subject	predicate

subject	predicate	comma	conjunction	subject	predicate

Connect two related simple sentences in a compound sentence with a semicolon.

Sara	practiced the trombone	;	Karen	practiced the violin.
subject	predicate	semicolon	subject	predicate

subject	predicate	semicolon	subject	predicate

subject	predicate	semicolon	subject	predicate

subject	predicate	semicolon	subject	predicate

Sentence Patterns *(cont.)*

2. Compound Sentences *(cont.)*

> **Use a semicolon and a conjunctive adverb** (or coordinating adverbial conjunction) **together in a compound sentence.**

<u>Sara</u>   <u>practiced the trombone</u>   <u>;</u>   **<u>however,</u>**   <u>Karen</u>   <u>practiced the violin.</u>

subject   predicate   semicolon &   subject   predicate

                                conjunctive adverb & comma

> **words often used as conjunctive adverbs** (or *coordinating adverbial conjunctions*)
>
> | | | | |
> |---|---|---|---|
> | accordingly, | consequently, | instead, | nonetheless, |
> | additionally, | for example, | likewise, | otherwise, |
> | also, | in addition, | meanwhile, | therefore, |
> | as a result, | indeed, | moreover, | thus, |
> | besides, | in fact, | nevertheless, | |

Simple Rule: Use a comma after a conjunctive adverb.

---

subject   predicate   semicolon &   subject   predicate
                          conjunctive adverb & comma

---

subject   predicate   semicolon &   subject   predicate
                          conjunctive adverb & comma

---

subject   predicate   semicolon &   subject   predicate
                          conjunctive adverb & comma

---

subject   predicate   semicolon &   subject   predicate
                          conjunctive adverb & comma

---

subject   predicate   semicolon &   subject   predicate
                          conjunctive adverb & comma

Sentence Patterns *(cont.)*

3. Complex Sentences

> **Connect independent clauses and dependent clauses to make a complex sentence.**

Independent Clause: has a subject and predicate

can stand alone and make sense

Dependent Clause: has a subject and predicate

has a subordinating conjunction

does not make sense without the independent clause

Sara	practiced the trombone	while	Karen	practiced the violin.
subject	predicate	subordinating conjunction	subject	predicate

(independent clause)   (subordinating conjunction and dependent clause)

An **independent clause** has a subject and a predicate and can stand alone as a sentence and make sense.

("Sara practiced the trombone" can stand alone and make sense.)

A **dependent clause** has a **subordinating conjunction** which makes it dependent upon another clause in order to make sense.

("while Karen practiced the violin" does **not** make sense alone.)

---

words often used as subordinating conjunctions

after	before	until	whether
although	even though	when	whether or not
as	rather than	whenever	while
as long as	since	where	if
because	unless	wherever	

---

subject	predicate	subordinating conjunction	subject	predicate

subject	predicate	subordinating conjunction	subject	predicate

subject	predicate	subordinating conjunction	subject	predicate

Sentence Patterns *(cont.)*

3. Complex Sentences: Punctuation Rules

Dependent Clause First:

When	the dependent clause comes first,	you must use a comma.
subordinating conjunction	dependent clause,	independent clause

subordinating conjunction	dependent clause,	independent clause

subordinating conjunction	dependent clause,	independent clause

subordinating conjunction	dependent clause,	independent clause

subordinating conjunction	dependent clause,	independent clause

Independent Clause First:

Do not use a comma	when	the independent clause comes first.
independent clause	subordinating conjunction	dependent clause

independent clause	subordinating conjunction	dependent clause

independent clause	subordinating conjunction	dependent clause

independent clause	subordinating conjunction	dependent clause

independent clause	subordinating conjunction	dependent clause

Name _____

Date _____

Writing Compound Sentences 1

Use conjunctions **and, but, or, nor, for, so,** and **yet** to connect two simple sentences together.

simple sentence with a simple predicate	comma plus conjunction	simple sentence with a simple predicate
	, and	

Name

Date

Writing Compound Sentences 2

Use conjunctions **and**, **but**, **or**, **nor**, **for**, **so**, and yet to connect two simple sentences together.
Write three drafts, improving each draft with more details as you write.

Subject and Predicate	Comma plus Conjunction		Subject and Predicate
Sandy danced,	and	Jamie played the piano.
Sandy danced in the center of the stage,	and	Jamie played music on the piano.
Sandy danced with some small children in the center of the stage,	and	Jamie played upbeat music on the piano in the background.

Name _____

Date _____

Writing Compound Sentences 3

"Buddy Clauses"

Words often used as coordinating adverbial conjunctions (<u>conjunctive adverbs</u>):

accordingly, additionally, also, as a result, besides, consequently, for example, for instance, furthermore, however, in addition, indeed, in fact, instead, likewise, meanwhile, moreover, nevertheless, nonetheless, otherwise, therefore, thus

Use coordinating adverbial conjunctions (<u>conjunctive adverbs</u>) from the above box to connect two independent clauses. Place a semicolon after the first clause, write the coordinating adverbial conjunction (<u>conjunctive adverb</u>) followed by a comma, and write a similar/related/equal clause. Be sure to use end marks.

Subject and Predicate	Semicolon	Coordinating Conjunction	Comma	Subject and Predicate similar to first subject and predicate
Harriet practiced the tuba	;	additionally	,	she did her homework assignments.

Writing Complex Sentences 1

"Bossy Clauses"

Subordinating conjunctions make one clause dependent on the other for meaning. Words often used as subordinating conjunctions: *after, although, as, as long as, because, before, even though, rather than, since, unless, until, when, whenever, where, wherever, whether, whether or not, while*

Use the pattern box below to write sentences that contain a *subordinating conjunction*, a *dependent clause*, a *comma*, and an *independent clause*. Two samples have been done for you. Make up ideas for sentences.

Rule: When the dependent clause comes first, *use a comma before the independent clause.*

Conjunction	Dependent Clause	Comma	Independent Clause
While	Sarah cleaned the whole apartment	,	Anna washed and waxed the car.
After	Sarah cleaned the whole apartment	,	Anna washed and waxed the car.

Name _____

Date _____

Writing Complex Sentences 2

"Bossy Clauses"

Subordinating conjunctions make one clause dependent on the other for meaning. Words often used as subordinating conjunctions:

after, although, as, as long as, because, before, even, though, rather than, since, unless, until, when, whenever, where, wherever, whether, whether or not, while

Use the pattern box below to write sentences that *contain an independent clause, a subordinating conjunction, and a dependent clause.* Do *not* use semicolon or commas *when the subordinating conjunction follows the independent clause.* Be sure to use end marks for each sentence.

Rule: When the independent clause comes first, do *not* use a comma.

Independent Clause	Subordinating Conjunction (no comma)	Dependent Clause
Sarah cleaned the whole apartment	while	Anna washed and waxed the car.

Animal Sentence Building

Directions: Make sentences using word clusters from each of the three columns. Have fun.

Elephants	are very flexible	but are hard to train.
Tigers from India	are large seal-like creatures	but have white feathers covering their heads.
Parrots	but must be treated with caution	and have a hard shell.
Monkeys	have large ears	that live in the jungle.
Dogs	have been beasts of burden	during rainy or cold seasons.
Cats	are primates	who serve as both pets and guards.
Ferrets	which in turn can be made into	butter, cheese, yogurt, and ice cream.
Manatees	make interesting and unusual pets,	to help it stay cool.
Bald eagles	that walk on all four feet	for centuries.
Horses	have stripes for camouflage	in mountainous regions.
Mice are nuisance animals	that prefer to live in the homes of people	to help them hunt.
Snakes are beneficial animals,	are not really bald,	who live in Florida's coastal waters.
Cows provide milk	that usually live in herds	with tails.
Antelope are deer-like animals	are magnificently colored birds	because they have many bones.
Turtles are reptiles	are domesticated animals	because they may be dangerous.

Introduction to Paragraph Writing

A paragraph is a group of related sentences that come together to form a complex thought. The paragraph is the basic building block of all essay, theme, story, and report writing. A paragraph that stands alone often has an attention-getter. Transitional devices—individual words and phrases—can link several related paragraphs to form essays, themes, stories, and reports. Stand-alone paragraphs have a beginning, middle, and ending. Paragraphs linked together in an essay or story often use the beginnings and endings of individual paragraphs as transitions.

Ten Types of Writing

Following are ten of commonly identified categories of writing: *description, narration, persuasion, information, comparison, journaling, poetry, music, story writing,* and *notes.*

Five Types of Paragraphs

These are five commonly identified types of paragraphs: *informative, narrative, persuasive, comparative,* and *descriptive.* Informative paragraphs provide facts. Narrative paragraphs usually tell of events in chronological order. Persuasive paragraphs attempt to get the reader to accept a point of view. Comparative paragraphs compare or contrast two items or ideas. Descriptive paragraphs use sensory, emotion, or movement words to provide description.

Two Types of Writers

Some students, especially those with strong verbal abilities and many experiences with print and reading, write with ease. Other students need much support in order to learn to write paragraphs. How can a teacher address both types of students in the same classroom?

Those with innate writing abilities probably write with ease just the same as they talk with ease. Exposure to good writing, to correct speech patterns, and to literature produces students who automatically write well. These students just "know" what looks and sounds good, but even those students may not have a conscious knowledge of the science of writing paragraphs. They have a feel for the *art* of writing but not the *science.* How do teachers deal with both types of students in the same classroom?

If You Want It, Model It!

Modeling paragraph writing is probably the single most important thing a teacher can do to help both the proficient and the at-risk writer. At-risk and proficient writers can both benefit from teacher modeling. Teachers need to model the writing process for all types of writing.

Chapter 4 features two modeled sequences for paragraph writing. The first sequence begins with a fully scripted and modeled paragraph of "How I Spent My Summer" (page 58) and is followed by guided lesson frames for "Awesome Birthday," "The Bad Grade," "The Journey," and "Dreaded Social Event." The second sequence begins with the fully scripted and modeled lesson for "Vacation" (page 82) and is followed by 22 guided lesson and planning frames, listed by title in the table of contents.

Introduction to Paragraph Writing *(cont.)*

Writing Assessment

First, *never* give a writing assignment and expect students to write one draft for a grade.

Writing is a process. Quality products require students to work through the writing process to develop that product.

Second, the teacher does not have to grade every dimension of writing for every assignment. If your students need practice in organization (*Plot and Plan* in this text), then model the process of organization until the students are ready for a guided session on organization. With one or more modeled and guided sessions, students begin to master organization. When the teacher thinks the students have mastered organization, then an assignment in organization may be given and a grade assigned.

Where to Begin?

Collect two or more colors of fine-point overhead markers. Make a transparency copy of the Winged Paragraph Planner on page 57 to introduce students to the parts of a paragraph: beginning, middle, and ending. Display it on an overhead projector. Do not distribute copies. This is a class model.

Point to the blank copy of Winged Paragraph Planner. Paragraphs have a central, main idea. Details surround the main idea. The ending of the paragraph is the conclusion.

Assignment Prompt: Write a paragraph that defines what a good friend is.

- Write the paragraph title—A Good Friend

- Ask students to turn the prompt into a main idea sentence.

- Accept suggestions. The teacher writes the main idea sentence in the center box.
  (Example: *A good friend is someone who is a friend in every circumstance.*)

- Ask students for suggestions for the supporting detail sentences.
  (Example: *A good friend will comfort me when I am in trouble, even if he thinks I was wrong.*)
  Write the sentence in the box.

- Lead students to develop a conclusion sentence.
  (Example: *Now that I have defined a good friend, it helps me know how to be a good friend to others.*)

- Lead students in reviewing each sentence for improvements in sentence structure, vocabulary, capitalization, punctuation, and spelling. Make corrections by over-writing on the transparency, using a different colored marker.

Winged Paragraph Planner

Name _____

Date _____

Title _____

3.

5.

7.

2.

4.

6.

1. Main Idea/Introductory Sentence

8. Ending/Concluding Sentence

Teacher Modeled Prompt-Response

How I Spent My Summer

Teacher Modeled Writing Lesson

In a modeled writing lesson, the teacher models every step of a lesson. Students observe and may participate orally, but the teacher writes and does think-aloud strategies.

Guided Writing Lesson

In a teacher-guided writing lesson, the teacher leads the students through each step of the lesson. Students do not go ahead of the class. Teachers use timing strategies to keep all students on the same step.

Teachers seek and give feedback to students during the guided writing lesson.

Prompt-Response Writing Lesson

A prompt-response frame is a table with two columns. The first column has prompts for each sentence of the paragraph. The student writes a response in the corresponding box of the second column. The prompt requires certain information and dictates what kind of sentence the student is to write. (See page 64.)

First, the teacher does a modeled prompt-response writing activity followed by a guided prompt-response activity.

Once the student has developed an understanding of the prompt-response activity, he or she can work independently, using the prompts in the prompt-response frame. The prompts still provide guidance for the student concerning overall structure, sequence, and sentence variety.

As students gain more confidence and skill, the teacher can ask students to develop prompts for the frame. Gradually, students take ownership of the concepts of paragraph structure and become independent writers who remember the elements of constructing a paragraph.

Getting Started

Materials

- two or more colors of fine-point overhead transparency markers
- transparency copies of "How I Spent My Summer" (pages 63–65) and "Revise and Edit Checklist" from chapter 1 (page 17) for the overhead projector
- alternative display methods: chart paper or electronic media

Plan Ahead

Make enough student copies of "The Day I Met My Best Friend" (pages 66 and 67) and "Revise and Edit Checklist." Do not distribute these yet.

Teacher Modeled Prompt–Response (cont.)

Modeling a Prompt-Response Writing Lesson

Say the following:

I am going to model a writing lesson called "How I Spent My Summer," using a prompt-response frame. In a modeled prompt-response writing lesson, students are not required to write but may contribute ideas to the lesson. The whole class will watch as I demonstrate writing a paragraph on a prompt-response frame.

First, look at the Prompt-Response Teacher Modeled Paragraph *(page 63)* on the overhead projector screen.

Before we start the writing process, I am going to do a "talk-through." It is an introduction to the prompt-response guided writing process. I will talk through the steps, but we will not make any plans and we will not write. This should take only two or three minutes. After that, I will demonstrate a modeled writing lesson.

Talk-Through: Introduction to Prompt-Response Guided Writing Lesson

Notice Step 1: Plot and Plan. On this page, we write the title, collect STAR vocabulary, collect ideas on a web, and transfer the ideas to the sequence list.

Notice Step 2: Package the First Draft *(page 64)*. That means we will take the ideas and vocabulary from the first page and write a paragraph.

Notice the frame with two columns. The first column says "Prompt," and the second column says "Response." The boxes in the prompt column contain specific instructions about the type of information and type of sentences required in the response boxes to the right. Each sentence has its own prompt and room for a response.

Notice Step 3: Prune and Plump below the frame. This is a revising process.

The prompt-response frame allows the student or the teacher a quick and easy way to look over the paragraph for errors. Each sentence is separated from the other sentences by the boxes. To revise a sentence, erase the one sentence and re-write the new one in its place. Another way to revise is to use a different colored pen and over-write on top of the first words.

To "prune" is to cut off or cut out. We might need to cut out unnecessary information or words.

To "plump" means to make fuller looking. We might need to add more information or more descriptive vocabulary to make a paragraph more interesting and meaningful.

Teacher Modeled Prompt–Response *(cont.)*

Notice Step 4: Polish and Re-Write.

We polish up the paragraph by checking the vocabulary choices against the check list to make sure we have made the paragraph interesting.

Then we check all punctuation. Look for end marks, commas, and other punctuation. Look for capitalization. Each box should have a capital letter at the beginning. Each proper noun needs a capital letter. Finally, check over the spelling. Ask a peer, the teacher, or check a dictionary for any uncertain words.

Once you are certain you have written an outstanding paragraph, you may re-write a final draft.

Use good handwriting so the work will be attractive to the reader.

Last, notice Step 5: Publish and Perform. Students may publish or perform the paragraphs in a variety of ways: add to a portfolio, display on a wall, read aloud to the class, read to a family member, read to the principal, read aloud at parent night, or publish in a school newspaper.

Modeled Prompt-Response Guided Writing Lesson

Now that you have heard about the prompt-response writing process, I am going to model a sample lesson for you. That means that I will do the writing while you observe and listen. After this modeled lesson, you will be required to write using the same methods I will model now.

Look again at the first transparency page of the lesson *(page 63)*.

Below Step 1: Plot and Plan, we see a space for a title. I will write the title "How I Spent My Summer" on the line and in the center of the web.

(Write the title on the line and in the center of the web.)

Step 1: Plot and Plan requires us to visualize the end product. The end product is going to be a paragraph about my summer.

We need to make a decision. Did the imaginary writer of this paragraph spend the entire summer in one place or in various places?

(Take student suggestions and lead the class in deciding which it is. The class may decide that the writer spent the entire summer at the beach. This would indicate that vocabulary development would center on summer at the beach.)

Part A is STAR vocabulary. Remember that the acronym STAR stands for sensory, technical, articulate, and realistic vocabulary.

We need to collect sensory words that reflect the places and activities the writer has experienced on vacation. Remember sensory words include five-senses words, emotion words, and movement words.

(Write student suggestions on the transparency.)

Teacher Modeled Prompt–Response *(cont.)*

We need technical words that reflect specific places or activities related to How I Spent My Summer. For example, if I went to NASA Space Camp, I might use technical terms like "ignition," "blast off," and "gravity."

(Write student suggestions on the transparency.)

We need articulate words. These include words that show time and space relationships and show transition.

(Write student suggestions on the transparency)

We need realistic words. For example, if you spent your summer in Australia, you might hear people refer to each other as "mate."

(Write student suggestions on the transparency)

During the writing lesson, you might think of other appropriate vocabulary words. It is acceptable to add other words to the vocabulary list during the writing process. Raise your hand if you have additional ideas.

Part B is Collect Ideas. We have decided where our imaginary writer spent the summer. We need to come up with six ideas about the kinds of things that could have happened during the summer.

(Write student suggestions on the transparency.)

Part C requires us to take the same six ideas and put them in a sequential order.

We can begin by looking at the web and deciding which event logically happened first.

(Put a small number one next to the choice on the web.)

Looking at the web, which event occurred first? I will transfer it to the Sequence Ideas List.

(Continue until you have all the items on the sequence list.)

Step 2: Package the First Draft is on the second transparency page *(page 64)*. We see the Prompt-Response frame. The prompt on the left tells us what information or what type of sentence goes in the response box on the right.

The first prompt tells us to write an attention-getting sentence. Attention-getting sentences attract the reader's attention. They work like an advertisement. Once the reader is interested, he or she may continue reading the whole paragraph.

The topic is, "How I Spent My Summer."

We could say I had a good summer. "Good" is a descriptive word. Is it a strong descriptive word? What word would be stronger?

(Accept suggestions.)

Teacher Modeled
Prompt–Response (cont.)

> ***A Well Planned Teachable Moment:*** Almost invariably, some student will use a very interesting word, phrase, or make up an extraordinary sentence.
>
> Take this opportunity to reward higher order vocabulary by making a show about the effective choice of vocabulary. Write the word and the student's name on a sticky note and stick it to the door. Tell that student he or she will receive a reward at the end of class. This will take only about 30 to 45 seconds, but it will leave a lasting impression on students about the value of higher vocabulary. Other students will copy the idea and use higher vocabulary—perhaps within the minute. Reward this frequently and the result will be a consciousness among students that higher vocabulary is important. This concern with words will transfer to writing.

(Write the class-developed attention-getting sentence in the box, using a fine point overhead marker.)

Next, we need to write a main idea sentence. The main idea sentence needs to convey to the reader the broad idea of how I spent my summer. All the ideas from the web will fit in the category of how I spent my summer. Like the attention-getting sentence, this sentence needs to be interesting. It will finish hooking the reader's attention.

(Accept student suggestions and lead the class in making a decision. Write the choice in the blank.)

The third prompt asks us to write a sentence about idea (a) from the Sequence Ideas List from page 1.

(Put transparency #1 on the overhead projector to see idea #1 again. Accept student suggestions. Select one sentence for the response frame.)

Continue reading the prompts for each item and lead students in developing response sentences.

Distribute Revise and Edit Checklists to students (page 17). Model reading through **Step 3:** Prune and Plump. Do think aloud strategy with the class as you check the paragraph against the list. Put check marks by satisfactory items and put a star by items that need work.

Make revisions on the transparency, using a different colored fine point marker as you lead the students through the checklist.

Step 4: Polish and Re-Write is a final opportunity to improve the writing. Check for well developed vocabulary usage using the STAR Check List. Check the Conventions of English Language list. Show students that it is easy to check for errors when sentences are separated on the frame.

Rewrite: Model re-writing the final draft on the third page of the transparency (page 65) of How I Spent My Summer.

Step 5: Publish and Perform

Lead the class in reading the final draft. Ask students to name ways they can publish and perform their writing.

How I Spent My Summer

(teacher modeled prompt-response paragraph)

(The teacher will model this lesson. For this modeled lesson, students observe the writing process. They may respond to the teacher's questions, but they do not write.)

Assignment: Write a made-up paragraph titled, "How I Spent My Summer."

Step 1: Plot and Plan

Title _____

A. STAR Vocabulary: (*List appropriate words under the headings below.*)

Sensory	Technical	Articulate	Realistic

B. Collect Ideas

C. Sequence Ideas List

(1) _____

(2) _____

(3) _____

(4) _____

(5) _____

(6) _____

How I Spent My Summer (cont.)

(teacher modeled prompt-response paragraph)

Step 2: Package the First Draft

Prompt	Response
Write an attention-getting sentence.	
Write a main idea sentence about the topic.	
Write a sentence about idea (1) from the sequence list.	
Write a compound sentence about idea (2) from the sequence list.	
Write a complex sentence about idea (3) from the sequence list.	
Write a simple sentence about idea (4) from the sequence list.	
Write a compound sentence about idea (5) from the sequence list.	
Write a sentence about idea (6) from the sequence list.	
Write a concluding sentence.	

Erase errors or use another color pen and over-write to make changes. Use the checklist the teacher provides for you to revise and edit the paragraph above.

Step 3: Prune and Plump (Remove unnecessary information. Add information.)

Step 4: Polish (Check and repair grammar, mechanics, and spelling.)

Step 5: Publish and Perform (Share your writing with others.)

How I Spent My Summer *(cont.)*

(teacher modeled prompt-response paragraph)

_____

Title (Rename the paragraph to make it more interesting to the reader)

_____

_____

_____

_____

_____

_____

_____

_____

_____

_____

_____

_____

_____

_____

_____

_____

_____

The Day I Met My Best Friend

(prompt-response guided paragraph 2)

Name_____   Date_____

Assignment: Your teacher will guide you through the basic paragraph below. Do not go ahead of the class.

Step 1: Plot and Plan

The Topic is _____

A. Collect STAR Vocabulary

Sensory	Technical	Articulate	Realistic

B. Collect Information

C. Sequence Information

(1) _____

(2) _____

(3) _____

(4) _____

(5) _____

(6) _____

The Day I Met My Best Friend *(cont.)*

(prompt-response guided paragraph 2)

Step 2: Package the First Draft

✔ Write the title on the title bar below.

✔ Remember to indent and write an attention-getting sentence on the first line.

✔ Write a main idea sentence about the topic.

✔ From list C, write a sentence about idea (1).

✔ Write a compound sentence about idea (2).

✔ Write a complex sentence about idea (3).

✔ Write a simple sentence about idea (4).

✔ Write a compound sentence about idea (5).

✔ Write a simple sentence about idea (6).

✔ Write a concluding sentence.

_____

Title

Attention-Getting Sentence	
Main Idea Sentence	
Idea (1)	
Idea (2)	
Idea (3)	
Idea (4)	
Idea (5)	
Idea (6)	
Concluding Sentence	

Step 3: Prune and Plump, Step 4: Polish and Re-Write, Step 5: Publish and Perform

Open Topic Practice Frame

(prompt-response guided paragraph 3)

Name_____ Date_____

Assignment: Your teacher will guide you through the basic paragraph below. Do not go ahead of the class.

Step 1: Plot and Plan

The Topic is _____

A. Collect STAR Vocabulary

Sensory	Technical	Articulate	Realistic

B. Collect Information

C. Sequence Information

(1) _____

(2) _____

(3) _____

(4) _____

(5) _____

(6) _____

Open Topic Practice Frame *(cont.)*

(prompt-response guided paragraph 3)

Step 2: Package the First Draft

- ✔ Write the title on the title bar below.
- ✔ Remember to indent and write an attention-getting sentence on the first line.
- ✔ Write a main idea sentence about the topic.
- ✔ From list C, write a sentence about idea (1).
- ✔ Write a compound sentence about idea (2).
- ✔ Write a complex sentence about idea (3).
- ✔ Write a simple sentence about idea (4).
- ✔ Write a compound sentence about idea (5).
- ✔ Write a simple sentence about idea (6).
- ✔ Write a concluding sentence.

Title

Attention-Getting Sentence	
Main Idea Sentence	
Idea (1)	
Idea (2)	
Idea (3)	
Idea (4)	
Idea (5)	
Idea (6)	
Concluding Sentence	

Step 3: Prune and Plump, Step 4: Polish and Re-Write, Step 5: Publish and Perform

Name_____   Date_____

Awesome Birthday
(narrative paragraph prompt-response frame)

Assignment: Write about a real or made-up birthday party that stands out in your mind.

STAR Vocabulary

Step 1: Plot and Plan

- Use the Prompt-Response frame to write sentences for the paragraph below.
- Use transitional words to lead the reader from one idea to another.
- Paint word pictures that make the reader feel involved.

Step 2: Package the First Draft

Prompt	Response
Write an introductory sentence that grabs the attention of the reader and introduces the main idea.	
Write a sentence that tells who was honored at the birthday party. Use adjectives to describe the person.	
Write a compound sentence that tells how the party was planned and who planned it. Be generous with details.	
Write a complex sentence that tells where and when the party took place. Use vivid description so the reader will be able to visualize the party.	
Write a sentence that tells the highlight of the party.	
Write about an incident that happened at the party.	
Write a closure sentence that lets the reader know the paragraph is finished. Closure can summarize, come to a conclusion, or re-state the introduction.	

Awesome Birthday *(cont.)*

Step 3: Prune and Plump

(student-teacher conference)

Use this checklist for revising the first draft.

_____ structure

_____ beginning, middle, ending

_____ clear main idea

_____ paragraphs present and correct

_____ clear sequence and flow of ideas

Sentences

_____ varied sentence beginnings

_____ mixed simple, compound, and complex sentences

_____ fluent and correct syntax

_____ Does the writing say what I intended to say?

_____ I can improve each sentence.

_____ I can complete unfinished details.

_____ I can add more description.

_____ I can correct obvious mistakes.

_____ I can think about what others say.

Personality

_____ conveys author's purpose

_____ sets mood and tone

_____ communicates with reader

_____ original and engaging

Step 4: Polish and Re-Write

(student-teacher or peer conference)

Use this checklist for revising the first draft.

STAR Vocabulary

Sensory

_____ five senses

_____ emotion

_____ movement

Technical

_____ specific to the topic

Articulate

_____ conveys clear meaning

_____ fluent

_____ transitional

_____ free of redundancy

_____ subject-verb agreement

_____ correctly used words

Realistic

_____ local vernacular

_____ cultural dialect

_____ appropriate phrases

_____ true to characters and situations

Conventions of English Language

_____ punctuation

_____ capitalization

_____ spelling

Write a Final Draft

_____
Title

_____

_____

_____

_____

_____

_____

_____

Step 5: Publish and Perform: Share with others.

Name_____　　Date_____

Good Impression

(narrative paragraph prompt-response frame)

Assignment: Write about a time you made a bad first impression on someone important. Tell how you later made a good impression and changed that person's mind about you. Write in first person, "I," and write in the past tense.	**STAR Vocabulary**

Step 1: Plot and Plan

- Use the prompt-response frame below to write sentences for your paragraph.
- Use transitional words to lead the reader from one idea to another.
- Use STAR vocabulary to paint word pictures that involve the reader.
- Write in the past tense.

Step 2: Package the First Draft

Prompt	Response
Beginning Write a question sentence that acts as an attention getter.	
Write a sentence that tells the topic of the paragraph.	
Middle Write a compound sentence telling who the important person was. Use descriptive words to tell how important the person was.	
When and where did you meet the person?	
What terrible act did you do to make such a bad impression? Paint word pictures and tell how you felt when you realized things were going badly.	
Write about the incident that made the person change his or her mind about you.	
Ending Describe the relationship you have with the person now.	

Good Impression *(cont.)*

Step 3: Prune and Plump
(student-teacher conference)

Use this checklist for revising the first draft.

Structure

_____ beginning, middle, ending

_____ clear main idea

_____ paragraphs present and correct

_____ clear sequence and flow of ideas

Sentences

_____ varied sentence beginnings

_____ mixed simple, compound, and complex sentences

_____ fluent and correct syntax

_____ Does the writing say what I intended to say?

_____ I can improve each sentence.

_____ I can complete unfinished details.

_____ I can add more description.

_____ I can correct obvious mistakes.

_____ I can think about what others say.

Personality

_____ conveys author's purpose

_____ sets mood and tone

_____ communicates with reader

_____ original and engaging

Step 4: Polish and Re-Write
(student-teacher or peer conference)

Use this checklist for revising the final draft.

STAR Vocabulary

Sensory

_____ five senses

_____ emotion

_____ movement

Technical

_____ specific to the topic

Articulate

_____ conveys clear meaning

_____ fluent

_____ transitional

_____ free of redundancy

_____ subject-verb agreement

_____ correctly used words

Realistic

_____ local vernacular

_____ cultural dialect

_____ appropriate phrases

_____ true to characters and situations

Conventions of English Language

_____ punctuation

_____ capitalization

_____ spelling

Write a Final Draft

_____
Title

_____

_____

_____

_____

_____

_____

_____

_____

Step 5: Publish and Perform (Share with others.)

Name_____   Date_____

The Bad Grade

(narrative paragraph prompt-response frame)

Assignment: Write a paragraph using the sentence prompts below to tell about a time you made a bad grade in school. Use the first person, "I," and write in the past tense.	**STAR Vocabulary**

Step 1: Plot and Plan

- Use the prompt-response frame below to write sentences for your paragraph.
- Use transitional words to lead the reader from one idea to another.
- Use STAR vocabulary to paint word pictures that involve the reader.
- Write in the past tense.

Step 2: Package the First Draft

Prompt	Response
Beginning Write an attention-grabbing sentence to hook the reader.	
Write an introductory sentence.	
Middle Write a compound sentence that tells why you made a bad grade.	
Write a complex sentence that tells when and where you made the bad grade.	
Write a sentence that tells what you did when you received the bad grade.	
Write a sentence that tells how you felt when you received the bad grade.	
Write two or more sentences that tell what you did after you received the bad grade.	
Ending Write a sentence that tells what you learned and what you did differently after the experience.	

The Bad Grade *(cont.)*

Step 3: Prune and Plump

(student-teacher conference)
Use this checklist for revising the first draft.

Structure
_____ beginning, middle, ending
_____ clear main idea
_____ paragraphs present and correct
_____ clear sequence and flow of ideas

Sentences
_____ varied sentence beginnings
_____ mixed simple, compound, and complex sentences
_____ fluent and correct syntax
_____ Does the writing say what I intended to say?
_____ I can improve each sentence.
_____ I can complete unfinished details.
_____ I can add more description.
_____ I can correct obvious mistakes.
_____ I can think about what others say.

Personality
_____ conveys author's purpose
_____ sets mood and tone
_____ communicates with reader
_____ original and engaging

Step 4: Polish and Re-Write

(student-teacher or peer conference)
Use this checklist for revising the final draft.

STAR Vocabulary
Sensory
_____ five senses
_____ emotion
_____ movement

Technical
_____ specific to the topic

Articulate
_____ conveys clear meaning
_____ fluent
_____ transitional
_____ free of redundancy
_____ subject-verb agreement
_____ correctly used words

Realistic
_____ local vernacular
_____ cultural dialect
_____ appropriate phrases
_____ true to characters and situations

Conventions of English Language
_____ punctuation
_____ capitalization
_____ spelling

Write a Final Draft

_____
Title

_____

_____

_____

_____

_____

_____

_____

_____

Step 5: Publish and Perform (Share with others.)

Name_____   Date_____

The Journey

(prompt-response narrative paragraph frame)

Assignment: Write a narrative paragraph about a journey you remember or imagine. Journeys sometimes have unexpected delays or problems. Use STAR vocabulary to create clear descriptions. Use transitions. Write in first person, "I," and use past tense.	**STAR Vocabulary**

Step 1: Plot and Plan

- Use the prompt-response frame below to write sentences for your paragraph.
- Use transitional words to lead the reader from one idea to another.
- Use STAR vocabulary to paint word pictures that involve the reader.

STEP 2: Package the First Draft

Prompt	Response
Beginning Write an attention-grabbing sentence to hook the reader.	
Write a simple main topic sentence.	
Middle Write a compound sentence that tells why you were traveling.	
Write a complex sentence that tells what you did to prepare for the trip.	
Write a complex sentence that tells two things that happened at once.	
Write two sentences that tell about the journey itself. What problems did you encounter?	
Write two sentences that give sensory descriptions such as sight, sound, and smell.	
Ending Write a sentence that tells how you feel about the journey.	

The Journey *(cont.)*

Step 3: Prune and Plump

(student-teacher conference)
Use this checklist for revising the first draft.

Structure

_____ beginning, middle, ending
_____ clear main idea
_____ paragraphs present and correct
_____ clear sequence and flow of ideas

Sentences

_____ varied sentence beginnings
_____ mixed simple, compound, and complex sentences
_____ fluent and correct syntax
_____ Does the writing say what I intended to say?
_____ I can improve each sentence.
_____ I can complete unfinished details.
_____ I can add more description.
_____ I can correct obvious mistakes.
_____ I can think about what others say.

Personality

_____ conveys author's purpose
_____ sets mood and tone
_____ communicates with reader
_____ original and engaging

Step 4: Polish and Re-Write

(student-teacher or peer conference)
Use this checklist for revising the final draft.

STAR Vocabulary

Sensory
_____ five senses
_____ emotion
_____ movement

Technical
_____ specific to the topic

Articulate
_____ conveys clear meaning
_____ fluent
_____ transitional
_____ free of redundancy
_____ subject-verb agreement
_____ correctly used words

Realistic
_____ local vernacular
_____ cultural dialect
_____ appropriate phrases
_____ true to characters and situations

Conventions of English Language

_____ punctuation
_____ capitalization
_____ spelling

Write a Final Draft

_____
Title

_____

_____

_____

_____

_____

_____

_____

_____

Step 5: Publish and Perform (Share with others.)

Name _____   Date _____

Dreaded Social Event

(narrative paragraph prompt-response frame)

Assignment: Write about a time you had to attend a social event that you dreaded, but discovered that you enjoyed it once you got there.

STAR Vocabulary

Step 1: Plot and Plan

- Use the prompt-response frame to write sentences for the paragraph below.

- Use transitional words to lead the reader from one idea to another.

- Paint word pictures that make the reader feel involved.

Step 2: Package the First Draft

Prompt	Response
Beginning Write an attention-grabbing sentence to get the reader interested.	
Write a sentence that tells what social event you dreaded. Tell who else would be there.	
Middle Write a compound sentence that tells why you dreaded the event.	
Write a compound sentence that tells what you did to avoid the experience and why you could not get out of going.	
Write a complex sentence that tells when and where the event took place.	
Write two or more sentences that tell about the event itself. Use vivid description.	
Write a sentence that tells about your surprise when you realized that you enjoyed the experience.	
Ending Write a sentence that tells how your thinking changed.	

Dreaded Social Event *(cont.)*

Step 3: Prune and Plump
(student-teacher conference)

Use this checklist for revising the first draft.

Structure

_____ beginning, middle, ending

_____ clear main idea

_____ paragraphs present and correct

_____ clear sequence and flow of ideas

Sentences

_____ varied sentence beginnings

_____ mixed simple, compound, and complex sentences

_____ fluent and correct syntax

_____ Does the writing say what I intended to say?

_____ I can improve each sentence.

_____ I can complete unfinished details.

_____ I can add more description.

_____ I can correct obvious mistakes.

_____ I can think about what others say.

Personality

_____ conveys author's purpose

_____ sets mood and tone

_____ communicates with reader

_____ original and engaging

Step 4: Polish and Re-Write
(student-teacher or peer conference)

Use this checklist for revising the final draft.

Star Vocabulary

Sensory

_____ five senses

_____ emotion

_____ movement

Technical

_____ specific to the topic

Articulate

_____ conveys clear meaning

_____ fluent

_____ transitional

_____ free of redundancy

_____ subject-verb agreement

_____ correctly used words

Realistic

_____ local vernacular

_____ cultural dialect

_____ appropriate phrases

_____ true to characters and situations

Conventions of English Language

_____ punctuation

_____ capitalization

_____ spelling

Write a Final Draft

_____

Title

_____

_____

_____

_____

_____

_____

_____

_____

_____

_____

Step 5: Publish and Perform (Share with others.)

Name_____   Date_____

Blank Prompt-Response Paragraph Frame

Assignment: Use the blank prompt-response frame to write your own prompts and sentences for the paragraph below.

STAR Vocabulary

Step 1: Plot and Plan

- Use transitional words to lead the reader from one idea to another.
- Paint word pictures that make the reader feel involved.

Step 2: Package the First Draft

Prompt	Response
Beginning	
Middle	
Ending	

Blank Prompt-Response Paragraph Frame *(cont.)*

Title:

Step 3: Prune and Plump
(student-teacher conference)
Use this checklist for revising the first draft.

Structure
_____ beginning, middle, ending
_____ clear main idea
_____ paragraphs present and correct
_____ clear sequence and flow of ideas

Sentences
_____ varied sentence beginnings
_____ mixed simple, compound, and complex sentences
_____ fluent and correct syntax
_____ Does the writing say what I intended to say?
_____ I can improve each sentence.
_____ I can complete unfinished details.
_____ I can add more description.
_____ I can correct obvious mistakes.
_____ I can think about what others say.

Personality
_____ conveys author's purpose
_____ sets mood and tone
_____ communicates with reader
_____ original and engaging

Step 4: Polish and Re-Write
(student-teacher or peer conference)
Use this checklist for revising the final draft.

Star Vocabulary
Sensory
_____ five senses
_____ emotion
_____ movement

Technical
_____ specific to the topic

Articulate
_____ conveys clear meaning
_____ fluent
_____ transitional
_____ free of redundancy
_____ subject-verb agreement
_____ correctly used words

Realistic
_____ local vernacular
_____ cultural dialect
_____ appropriate phrases
_____ true to characters and situations

Conventions of English Language
_____ punctuation
_____ capitalization
_____ spelling

Write a Final Draft

_____
Title

_____
_____
_____
_____
_____
_____
_____
_____

Step 5: Publish and Perform (Share with others.)

Teacher Modeled Paragraph

Vacation

Guided Paragraph Planner

This teacher section will guide you through a teacher-modeled lesson and a guided lesson. Modeled lessons allow the student to see and hear the process of writing. Guided writing provides a scaffold for students as they learn and participate in the writing process. Begin by giving complete support as students learn strong writing process skills. Gradually, students will master the process and will not need support.

Modeling a Lesson

Do not distribute student copies for a class-modeled paragraph. Students will watch as the teacher models the steps to planning and writing a paragraph.

If you want it, teach it! Help students plan very thoroughly, and they will have little that needs to be revised or edited. Stress the importance of planning.

Materials: Overhead projector, transparency copy of Vacation Guided Paragraph Planner (page 88) and STAR Vocabulary planner from chapter 2 (page 22), fine-point overhead projection markers

Model: Model all of the steps below using think-aloud strategy and eliciting class participation.

Step 1: Plot and Plan

Say the following:

A paragraph is a group of sentences that have a common main idea that binds them together.

All the people in the Smith family belong together under the Smith name. They are related to each other, and each person is an important member of the family. Paragraphs are like sentence families.

For this lesson, the class will participate in writing about an imaginary beach vacation. First, we need to brainstorm vocabulary related to the beach and to a beach vacation.

- Display the STAR vocabulary planner and review the terms related to collecting vocabulary for a topic using the STAR vocabulary model: sensory, technical, articulate, and realistic.
- Take student suggestions for beach and beach vacation-related vocabulary. Write those words on the STAR vocabulary overhead transparency.

Suggestions:

You may substitute large chart paper for writing the vocabulary to display in the classroom. Later, type the STAR vocabulary list and distribute copies for students' writing binders. Direct students' attention to the overhead transparency of Vacation Guided Paragraph Planner.

Say:

Notice the small STAR vocabulary planner on this page. Always plan vocabulary lists in advance. This is a small list. Are there words from the four-column STAR list we absolutely want to include?

(Take student ideas and write those words on the small list.)

Teacher Modeled Paragraph *(cont.)*

Vacation

Step 1: Plot and Plan *(cont.)*

Teaching Focus: Collecting Ideas

Collect ideas on the Idea Collection Web in the center of the page. Write on the overhead transparency, a whiteboard, or a large chart paper. Collect ideas about six things that could happen during a beach vacation.

Say:

Always collect ideas on a graphic organizer. This lesson will require us to use a web. We need to collect a minimum of six ideas for things that might happen on a beach vacation.

(Take student suggestions and write them on the web.)

Teaching Focus: Sequencing the Ideas

Say:

Look at the web and decide which thing probably happened first.

(Write the student selection on line one.)

Continue this discussion until the class has decided on an order for the Sequence Ideas list. Write those items from the web onto the sequence list on the overhead transparency.

Teaching Focus: Planning Transitional Vocabulary

Say:

In order for the reader to be able to understand that things happened in a certain order, we use transitional words such as *first, next, last, meanwhile, afterwards, last,* and *consequently.* For this exercise, we will use a transitional word for each event. Which word is appropriate for introducing the event for line one on the Sequence Ideas List?

(Take student suggestions and write them on the transition list in front of each item.)

Step 2: Package the First Draft

Teaching Focus: Attention-Getting Sentence

Say:

Writers must compete with millions of other writers in order to get their work read. Writers must "sell" their work to the reader to get the reader to "buy into" reading the paragraph. Readers scan over books, newspaper stories, magazines, and other written works. The ones that get their attention quickly are read.

Newspaper headlines are examples of selling a story to readers. The title or attention-getting sentence is the advertisement to get readers to read the story.

Questions make good attention-getting sentences.

Sample attention-getting question: Have you ever been on a good vacation?

"Good" is a very ordinary word. Is there a more interesting word than "good" for the attention-getting sentence?

Teacher Modeled Paragraph *(cont)*

Vacation

Step 2: Package the First Draft *(cont.)*

(Take suggestions—e.g., *awesome, unforgettable, wonderful,* etc. Substitute suggested words in the sentence, "Have you ever been on an unforgettable vacation?")

Say:

Startling statements make good attention-getting sentences.

Example: "I hate beach vacations!"

(Take student suggestions for startling statements for the attention-getter. Guide the class to select a question or startling statement for the attention-getting sentence and write it on the first line.)

> Teaching Focus: Main Idea or Thesis Sentence

Say:

The main idea is like an umbrella. All the details must be able to stand under the umbrella together with other similar sentences. The sentences must all have a common bond.

(Take suggestions for main-idea sentences about the beach vacation. Have the class select the most appropriate sentence.)

> Teaching Focus: Supporting Detail Sentences

Say:

Look at the first item on the sequence list. What would be a good sentence about item one on the list? Remember to use the transitional word we have selected in the sentence.

(Take suggestions for sentences about the first item on the list. Remind students to use the transitional word in front of the item number. After accepting several ideas for the first sentence, guide the class to select the best one. Ask students to read over the sentence and see if a better vocabulary word or phrase might improve the sentence. Remind students of the STAR Vocabulary list on the left.)

> Teaching Focus: Sentence Types

Say:

There are three basic sentence types: simple, compound, and complex. Good writers use varied sentences.

Simple Sentence: One subject, one predicate ("First, we arrived at the beach hotel in the evening.")

Compound Sentence: One subject, one predicate, conjunction, one subject, one predicate. ("First, we arrived at the beach hotel in the evening, and then we ran to the beach to swim.")

Complex Sentence: one subject and predicate dependant on the other subject and predicate ("First, we arrived at the beach hotel in the evening while a concert was playing.")

Teacher Modeled Paragraph (cont.)

Vacation

Step 2: Package the First Draft *(cont.)*

Say:

What kind of sentence did we use for the first detail sentence? (**Receive responses.**) We need to vary the sentence for detail two from the Sequence Ideas List.

Look at idea two and think of a sentence with a different structure. (**Receive responses.**)

Teaching Focus: Sentence Sequencing

Guide students one sentence at a time through the entire sequence list.

Teaching Focus: Concluding Sentence

Say:

We have written a sentence about each idea in the Sequence Ideas List. Now we need to write a concluding sentence so the reader will know the paragraph is finished.

Concluding sentences do one or more of the following:

* summarize
* conclude based on the evidence
* restate the main idea by using different words.

(Take student suggestions for a concluding sentence. Ask the class to select the best concluding sentence.)

Step 3: Prune and Plump

Teaching Focus: Revising and Editing

Guide students to read over the entire paragraph to see if it makes sense. Then go through each item on the Revise and Edit Checklist from page 17 to see if the paragraph needs improvement.

Students will see that good planning guided them through the development of a quality paragraph.

Remind students to check the work for inclusion of words from the STAR Vocabulary List and from the Sequence Ideas List.

Make any editing corrections using a different color fine-point marker and write directly on top of the transparency sheet.

Re-write a revised copy in front of the class. Think aloud and ask students to make suggestions.

Step 4: Polish and Re-Write

Teaching Focus: Final Editing and Polishing

Explain to students that they will now use the Revise and Edit Checklist again to write a final polished and edited copy of their work.

Teacher Modeled Paragraph (cont)

Vacation

Step 5: Publish and Perform

Teaching Focus: Presentation

Ask students to appraise the finished product.

Let individual students read the paragraph aloud. Lead the class in a choral reading of the paragraph. Have students make individual copies of the complete, revised paragraph and post them.

De-brief students: Ask them to repeat the writing process steps and tell what they learned about the writing process. Ask for other comments.

If you are teaching students word processing on computer software, using a class-created paragraph both reinforces the writing process and allows the students to concentrate on the task of typing and word processing.

Guided Student Lesson

Say:

I will guide you through individual lessons like the modeled lesson, but you will have time limits to write each sentence.

Each student in the class will be writing on the same sentence assignment at the same time, but each student will write individual responses on his or her own sheet. Each one of you will write about a real trip you remember.

(Distribute student copies of STAR Vocabulary from chapter 2 and Vacation Guided Paragraph Planner on page 88 for students to plan and write their own paragraphs. Do not distribute teacher directions.)

Say:

First, think of a vacation you remember. (Example: a camping trip including white water rafting)

Look at the STAR Vocabulary sheet. Write sensory words that you think of when you remember this vacation. In order to select these words, remember the five senses, movement, and emotions (e.g., scary, screech-owl hoots, campfire smell, bacon frying smell, wet, churning around, fast). You have two minutes.

Write technical words that you think of when you remember this vacation. These are words that would probably only be related to a vacation at the place you are thinking about (for example, "forest ranger," "bears," "campfire," "tent," "camper," "white-water rafting.")

Continue leading students to develop the (A)rticulate list and the (R)ealistic list on STAR Vocabulary.

Teacher Modeled Paragraph (cont.)

Vacation

Guided Student Lesson (cont.)

Guide students through each step. Do not let students work ahead. Refer to the model lesson and follow the frame on the student sheet titled "Vacation."

Time limits keep students motivated and on track. Adjust time limits as needed to assure all students can finish. For example, say, "You have 60 seconds to write the attention-getting sentence."

Observe students to see if they need a few more seconds. Say, "Who needs 30 more seconds?" Train students to answer by raising a hand and not talking.

As your students work through the process, ask orally for sample sentences. This oral reinforcement will keep students on track and give you valuable assessment information. Lead students through the entire paragraph using the writing process from the modeled lesson.

Use the Guided Paragraph Planner model for teaching the following writing assignments: "Vacation," "I'm Late," "Convince Me!" "Horse Feathers," "Roller Coaster Emotions," "The Big Argument," and "A Tribute."

The planning frames and graphic organizers (pages 95–112) which follow the above listed writing assignments in chapter 4 provide a rich supply of specific and open-topic lessons which allow the teacher to guide all students to self-confidence and mastery in paragraph writing. Other lesson titles include: "How Do You Do?" "Narrative Paragraph," "Five Questions," "All About Apples," "Use Your Senses," "Two Pets," "Write a Credo," "Three Stellar Friends," "Blue Ribbon Events," and "Power to Cure."

> **Remove the scaffold a little at a time. As your students gain skills, do less guiding and give students more responsibility for completing the assigned paragraphs.**

Vacation

Guided Paragraph Planner

Name_____   Date_____

Your teacher will guide you through the basic paragraph below. Do not go ahead of the class.

1. Plot and Plan

The topic is _____

STAR Vocabulary	**Collection Web**	**Sequence Ideas List**
Brainstorm appropriate vocabulary on the lines below.	Collect thoughts and ideas on the web below.	Use the sequence list to put the ideas in order. Add transitional words in front of the numbers.

Sequence Ideas List:

First, 1. _____
_____ 2. _____
_____ 3. _____
_____ 4. _____
_____ 5. _____
_____ 6. _____

2. Package the First Draft

(A) Write an attention-getting sentence. (B) Write a main idea sentence. (C) In order, write six sentences for the six ideas in the Sequence Ideas List above. Use a mixture of simple, compound, and complex sentences. Use vivid words from the vocabulary list. (D) Write a concluding sentence.

Title _____

_____

_____

_____

_____

_____

_____

_____

_____

_____

3. Prune and Plump: Use the Revise and Edit Checklist from Chapter 4 (page 81) to guide revisions.

4. Polish and Re-Write: Use Revise and Edit Checklist from Chapter 4 (page 81) to guide editing.

5. Publish and Perform: Print a copy, store electronically, share, or read aloud.

I'm Late!

Guided Paragraph Planner

Name_____   Date_____

1. **Plot and Plan**

   Use the graphic organizer below to collect ideas for a paragraph about when you were late for an appointment, an event, or school. Use ideas from the STAR Vocabulary list on the left. Add your own words. Be sure to tell what things caused you to be late and tell what happened because you were late. After collecting ideas on the web, put them in order under the Sequence Ideas column and insert transitional words under the Transition column. Make the paragraph real and vivid to the reader. Use transitional words and write introductory and concluding sentences. Use sentence variety.

STAR Vocabulary		**Collect Ideas**	**Sequence Ideas**

afterwards	overslept
consequent	thrilled
behind	frightened
concurrent	early
consecutive	prompt
angry	timely
subsequent	postponed
lost	dilatory
hurried	punctual
fault	lengthy
detained	fleeting
delayed	crawling

Transition

_____ 1._____
_____
_____ 2._____
_____
_____ 3._____
_____
_____ 4._____
_____
_____ 5._____
_____
_____ 6._____
_____

2. **Package the First Draft:** Write an introductory sentence followed by a sentence about each idea in the sequence list you created. Write a concluding sentence at the end. Use the back of this page if needed.

   _____

   _____

   _____

   _____

   _____

   _____

   _____

3. **Prune and Plump:** Remove unnecessary information and add needed information.

4. **Polish and Re-Write:** Edit for grammar, punctuation, and spelling and write a final draft.

5. **Publish and Perform:** Print a copy, store electronically, share, or read aloud.

Convince Me!

Guided Paragraph Planner

Name_____   Date_____

1. Plot and Plan

Use the graphic organizer below to collect ideas for a paragraph persuading someone to grant you a special privilege. Use ideas from the STAR Vocabulary list below. Add your own words. Be sure to tell why you want the privilege, why you are worthy of it, and what will happen once you are granted the special privilege. After collecting ideas on the web, put them in order under the Sequence Ideas column and insert transitional words under the Transition column. Make the paragraph real and vivid to the reader. Use transitional words and write introductory and concluding sentences. Use sentence variety.

STAR Vocabulary   **Collect Ideas**   **Sequence Ideas**

moment	fortunate
chance	favorable time
opportunity	necessary
satisfy	important
influence	assure
sway	prevail upon
prove	recognition
praise	gratitude
trustworthy	persuade
honor	_____
lucky	_____
timing	_____

Transition

_____1._____
_____
_____2._____
_____
_____3._____
_____
_____4._____
_____
_____5._____
_____
_____6._____
_____

2. Package the First Draft:
Write an introductory sentence followed by a sentence about each idea in the sequence list you created. Write a concluding sentence at the end. Use the back of this page if needed.

_____

_____

_____

_____

_____

_____

_____

3. Prune and Plump:
Remove unnecessary information and add needed information.

4. Polish and Re-Write:
Edit for grammar, punctuation, and spelling and write a final draft.

5. Publish and Perform:
Print a copy, store electronically, share, or read aloud.

Horse Feathers!

Guided Paragraph Planner

Name _____   Date _____

1. Plot and Plan

Use the graphic organizer below to collect ideas for a paragraph that tells about something as preposterous as a horse having feathers. Use ideas from the STAR Vocabulary list below or make your own list. Then, put the ideas in a logical order on the sequence list. Remember to use introductory and concluding sentences. Use sentence variety. This is a good opportunity for comedic writing.

STAR Vocabulary		Collect Ideas	Sequence Ideas
preposterous	ridiculous		1. _____
ludicrous	absurd		2. _____
fatuous	foolish		3. _____
silly	asinine		4. _____
stupid	inane		5. _____
nonsensical	laughable		6. _____
irrational	unreasonable		
bizarre	_____		
_____	_____		

2. Package the First Draft

Write an introductory sentence followed by a sentence about each idea in the sequence list you created. Write a concluding sentence at the end.

_____

_____

_____

_____

_____

_____

_____

3. Prune and Plump: Remove unnecessary information and add needed information.

4. Polish and Re-Write: Edit for grammar, punctuation, and spelling and write a final copy.

5. Publish and Perform: Print a copy, store electronically, share, or read aloud.

Roller Coaster Emotions

Guided Paragraph Planner

Name _____   Date _____

1. Plot and Plan

Use the graphic organizer below to collect ideas for a paragraph about when your emotions went from one extreme to another. Use ideas from the STAR Vocabulary list on the left. Add your own words. Be sure to tell what events caused you to be so emotional. After collecting ideas on the web, put them in order under the Sequence Ideas column and insert transitional words under the Transition column. Make the paragraph real and vivid to the reader. Use transitional words and write introductory and concluding sentences. Use sentence variety.

STAR Vocabulary   **Collect Ideas**   **Sequence Ideas**

sad	motivated
guilty	depressed
excited	thrilled
love	hate
happy	envious
hopeful	joyous
ecstatic	angry
grief	vengeful
victorious	_____
morbid	_____
_____	_____
_____	_____

Transition

_____ 1. _____
       _____
_____ 2. _____
       _____
_____ 3. _____
       _____
_____ 4. _____
       _____
_____ 5. _____
       _____
_____ 6. _____
       _____

2. Package the First Draft:
Write an introductory sentence followed by a sentence about each idea in the sequence list you created. Write a concluding sentence at the end. Use the back of the page if needed.

_____

_____

_____

_____

_____

_____

_____

_____

3. Prune and Plump: Remove unnecessary information and add needed information.

4. Polish and Re-Write: Edit for grammar, punctuation, and spelling and write a final draft.

5. Publish and Perform: Print a copy, store electronically, share, or read aloud.

The Big Argument

Guided Paragraph Planner

Name_____   Date_____

1. Plot and Plan

Use the graphic organizer below to collect ideas for a paragraph about a time you had an argument with someone. Be sure to tell what caused the argument. Use ideas from the STAR Vocabulary list below. Add your own words. After collecting ideas on the web, put them in order under the Sequence Ideas column and insert transitional words under the Transition column. Make the paragraph real and vivid to the reader. Write introductory and concluding sentences. Use sentence variety.

STAR Vocabulary		Collect Ideas	Sequence Ideas

STAR Vocabulary		
sad	spiteful	
guilty	depressed	
excited	thrilled	
love	hate	
happy	envious	
hopeful	joyous	
ecstatic	angry	
grief	vengeful	
hurried	_____	
fault	_____	
victorious	_____	
morbid	_____	

Transition

_____1._____
_____
_____2._____
_____
_____3._____
_____
_____4._____
_____
_____5._____
_____
_____6._____
_____

2. Package the First Draft
Write an introductory sentence followed by a sentence about each idea in the sequence list you created. Write a concluding sentence at the end. Use the back of this page if needed.

_____
_____
_____
_____
_____
_____
_____
_____
_____

3. Prune and Plump:
Remove unnecessary information and add needed information.

4. Polish and Re-Write:
Edit for grammar, punctuation, and spelling and write a final draft.

5. Publish and Perform:
Print a copy, store electronically, share, or read aloud.

A Tribute

Guided Paragraph Planner

Name_____   Date_____

1. Plot and Plan

Use the graphic organizer below to collect ideas for a paragraph that pays tribute to a person you know.   Use ideas from the STAR Vocabulary list below. Add your own words. Be sure to tell why you consider this person worthy of tribute. How has the person affected your life or the lives of others? After collecting ideas on the web, put them in order under the Sequence Ideas column and insert transitional words under the Transition column. Make the paragraph real and vivid to the reader. Write introductory and concluding sentences. Use sentence variety.

STAR Vocabulary		Collect Ideas	Sequence Ideas

STAR Vocabulary

honor	respect
esteem	gratitude
praise	acknowledgement
compliment	recognition
eulogy	commendation
memorial	testimonial
extolling	laudation

Collect Ideas

Sequence Ideas

Transition

_____1._____
      _____
_____2._____
      _____
_____3._____
      _____
_____4._____
      _____
_____5._____
      _____
_____6._____
      _____

2. Package the First Draft:
Write an introductory sentence followed by a sentence about each idea in the sequence list you created. Write a concluding sentence at the end. Use the back of this page if needed.

_____

_____

_____

_____

_____

_____

_____

3. Prune and Plump:
Remove unnecessary information and add needed information.

4. Polish and Re-Write:
Edit for grammar, punctuation, and spelling and write a final draft.

5. Publish and Perform:
Print a copy, store electronically, share, or read aloud.

Guided Paragraph Planner Blank

Name_____   Date_____

Title: _____

Prompt: _____

1. Plot and Plan

STAR Vocabulary	**Collect Ideas**	**Sequence Ideas**
Brainstorm appropriate vivid vocabulary on the vocabulary planner.	Collect thoughts and ideas on the web below.	Use the sequence list to put the ideas in order.

Transition

_____   1. _____
_____   2. _____
_____   3. _____
_____   4. _____
_____   5. _____
_____   6. _____
_____   7. _____
_____   8. _____

2. Package the First Draft

Use a mixture of simple, compound, and complex sentences to write a paragraph. Remember to use STAR vocabulary. (A) Write an attention-getting sentence. (B) Write a main idea sentence introducing the main idea of the prompt. (C) Write eight sentences using each idea in order from the sequence list. (D) Write a concluding sentence.

Title _____

_____
_____
_____
_____
_____
_____
_____
_____
_____
_____
_____
_____

3. Prune and Plump   4. Polish and Re-Write   5. Publish and Perform

Guided Paragraph Planner Blank *(cont.)*

Name_____   Date_____

1. **Plot and Plan:** Your teacher will assign a topic for this paragraph. Develop a STAR Vocabulary list. Create a web to collect ideas and then put the ideas on a sequence list. Use the list to guide you as you write the paragraph.

2. **Write a First Draft**

   Beginning: Write a sentence that introduces the topic. Use capitals and periods. Indent the first word.

   _____

   _____

   _____

   _____

   Middle: Write three or more sentences about the topic. Begin each sentence differently. Write at least one simple, one compound, and one complex sentence.

   _____

   _____

   _____

   _____

   _____

   _____

   _____

   _____

   _____

   _____

   _____

   Ending: Write one or more sentences to end the paragraph. The reader will know the paragraph is finished by the way these sentences close the topic. Do not indent.

   _____

   _____

   _____

   _____

   _____

3. **Prune and Plump**   4. **Polish and Re-Write**   5. **Publish and Perform**

How Do You Do?

Name_____   Date_____

Directions: Think of something you know how to do and write the directions for your class. Follow the format below.

How to_____

Step 1: Plot and Plan

  A. Gather these ingredients, supplies, or materials.   B. Gather these tools.

  _____   _____   _____

  _____   _____   _____

  _____   _____   _____

  _____   _____   _____

  C. Create a web of all the steps.   D. Put the steps in correct order.

  1. _____

  _____

  2. _____

  _____

  3. _____

  _____

  4. _____

  _____

  5. _____

  _____

Step 2: Package the First Draft

  _____

_____

_____

_____

_____

_____

_____

_____

_____

_____

Step 3: Prune and Plump   **Step 4: Polish and Re-Write**   **Step 5: Publish and Perform**

If more space is needed, write on the back of this page.

Narrative Paragraph

Name_____   Date_____

Step 1: Plot and Plan

Write a narrative paragraph that describes an event you participated in or witnessed. Before writing, use the sequential planner below to plan the order of details for your paragraph.

Sequential Planner →

1.	2.	3.	4.

5.	6.	7.	8

When writing sentences, use some of the *transitional* words from the lists below.

Time-Order Transitional words.

first	second	always	then
next	later	eventually	soon
before	last	meanwhile	next week
after that	while	during	afterwards

Cause-and-Effect Transitional words

since	because	this
therefore	accordingly	due to
as a consequence		so
for this reason	if . . . then	as a result

Step 2: Package the First Draft: Write simple, compound, and complex sentences.

Title _____

_____

_____

_____

_____

_____

_____

_____

_____

_____

_____

_____

_____

_____

Step 3: Prune and Plump   **Step 4: Polish and Re-Write**   **Step 5: Publish and Perform**

Five Questions

Name_____   Date_____

Practice: Answer the "w" questions (who, what, when, where, why) to create a paragraph in this transitional frame.

On _____ , we had a surprise dinner party
                when

at _____ . _____ , _____
      where   who   who

and, _____ came, too. We held the dinner party because it
                who

was _____ . We were very sneaky about how we planned the dinner.
             why

First, we _____.
                            what

Then we _____.
                            what

Finally, we _____.
                            what

Step 1: Plot and Plan: Directions: Create a web and answer "w" questions about a real or imagined picnic.

Step 2: Package the First Draft _____

_____

_____

_____

_____

_____

_____

_____

_____

_____

_____

_____

_____

Step 3: Prune and Plump   **Step 4: Polish and Re-Write**   **Step5: Publish and Perform**

All About Apples

Name_____   Date_____

Step 1: Plot and Plan

STAR Vocabulary: Hold a real apple in your hand. Use the five senses to brainstorm words that describe an apple. Be creative and imagine the apple raw and cooked in various recipes. Write words that describe apples in each column below.

Sight	Sound	Taste	Touch	Smell

Use the vocabulary and graphic organizer above to write a paragraph that describes apples. Remember introductory and concluding sentences, capitals, end marks, and indentions for paragraphs. Ask a classmate to peer-edit the paragraph with you. Make five improvements.

Step 2: Package the First Draft

_____

_____

_____

_____

_____

_____

_____

_____

_____

_____

_____

_____

_____

Step 3: Prune and Plump   **Step 4: Polish and Re-Write**   **Step 5: Publish and Perform**

On the back of this page, draw and write a newspaper advertisement that persuades people to try your brand of apples.

Use Your Senses

Name_____   Date_____

Step 1: Plot and Plan

STAR Vocabulary: Hold a real object in your hand, such as a seashell. Use the five senses to brainstorm words that describe the object. Be creative and imagine the object in different settings or for different uses. Write words that describe the object in each column below.

Sight	Sound	Taste	Touch	Smell

Use the vocabulary and graphic organizer above to write a paragraph that describes the object. Imagine a new and creative use for the object. Remember to indent the first sentence of the paragraph, use capitals, and use end marks.

Step 2: Package the First Draft

_____

_____

_____

_____

_____

_____

_____

_____

_____

_____

_____

_____

_____

_____

Step 3: Prune and Plump   Step 4: Polish and Re-Write   Step 5: Publish and Perform

On the back, draw and write a newspaper advertisement that persuades people to buy this object from you and use it in this new way.

Two Pets

Name_____   Date_____

Step 1: Plot and Plan Prompt: You want to buy two exotic pets from the pet store. Use the graphic organizer to name the pets and collect details about why each would make a good pet. Develop a STAR Vocabulary list. Write one paragraph about each potential pet. Remember each paragraph must have a beginning, middle, and ending.

STAR Vocabulary

_____
_____
_____
_____
_____
_____
_____
_____
_____

Step 2: Package the First Draft

_____
_____
_____
_____
_____
_____
_____
_____
_____
_____
_____
_____
_____
_____
_____
_____

Step 3: Prune and Plump   **Step 4: Polish and Re-Write**   **Step 5: Publish and Perform**

Compare and Contrast 1

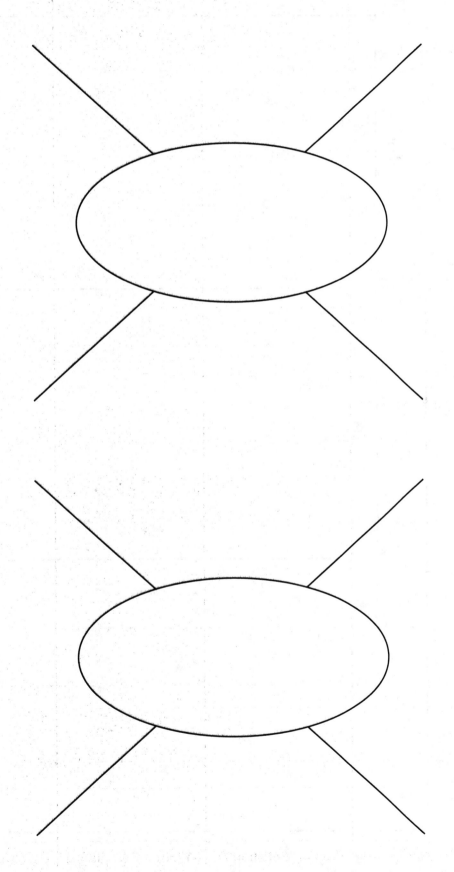

Compare and Contrast 2

Name _____

Date _____

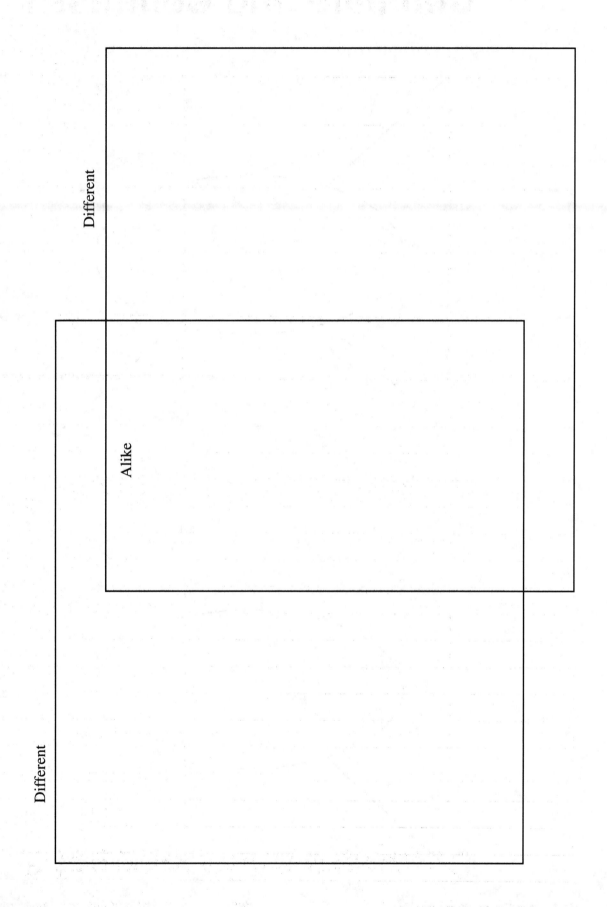

Different

Alike

Different

Compare and Contrast 3

Name_____   Date_____

_____
_____
_____
_____
_____
_____
_____
_____
_____
_____
_____
_____
_____
_____
_____
_____
_____
_____
_____

Comparison Chart

Name_____   Date_____

Write a Credo

Name_____   Date_____

Write Three Related Paragraphs   ## STAR Vocabulary

- **Discuss:** democracy, freedom, and human rights with your classmates.
- **Vocabulary:** make a related STAR Vocabulary word list.
- **Assignment:** Plan three related paragraphs that define what you think about democracy, freedom, and human rights. What would you put into a new civilization if you were the designer?

_____

_____

_____

_____

_____

_____

_____

_____

1. I stand for these principles:

2. I will not stand for these things:

3. If designing a civilization, I would do these things:

Write a Credo (cont.)

Name_____ Date_____

I stand for these principles: _____

_____

_____

_____

_____

_____

_____

_____

I will not stand for the following: _____

_____

_____

_____

_____

_____

_____

_____

_____

If I were designing a civilization, I would_____

_____

_____

_____

_____

_____

_____

_____

Three Stellar Friends

Name_____   Date_____

Write Three Related Paragraphs

1. Plot and Plan

Assignment: Write three related paragraphs. Choose three of your friends and write a paragraph about each. Collect information on the three star graphic organizers below. Write the name in the center and collect information on the points and outside lines. You may write good things only.

2. Package the First Draft

On your own paper, write one paragraph about each of the three friends you named on the stars.

3. Prune and Plump

Use Step 3: Prune and Plump from the Revise and Edit guide sheet your teacher supplies. With a teacher or peer, read what you have written. Put a check beside those items that are satisfactory. Put a star beside those items that need revising. Erase and re-write only those items that need revising or use a different colored pen to over-write directly on the first draft.

4. Polish and Re-Write

Ask a peer to read your paper and make suggestions for STAR Vocabulary improvements and English standards.

5. Publish and Perform

Blue Ribbon Events

Name_____   Date_____

Write Three Related Paragraphs

1. Plot and Plan

Assignment: Write three related paragraphs. Choose three blue ribbon events from your life and write about each one. Collect information on the three blue ribbon graphic organizers below. Name the event in the center and collect information on the other sections.

2. Package the First Draft

On your own paper, write one paragraph about each of the three blue ribbon events of your life.

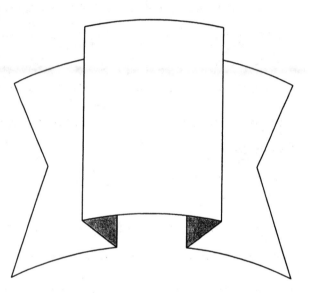

3. Prune and Plump

Use Step 3: Prune and Plump from the Revise and Edit guide sheet your teacher supplies. With a teacher or peer, read what you have written. Put a check beside those items that are satisfactory. Put a star beside those items that need revising. Erase and re-write only those items that need revising or use a different colored pen to over-write directly on the first draft.

4. Polish and Re-Write

Ask a peer to read your paper and make suggestions for STAR Vocabulary improvements and English standards.

5. Publish and Perform

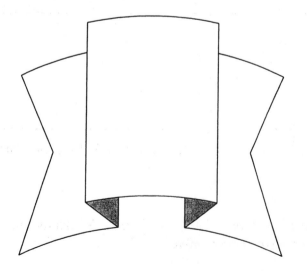

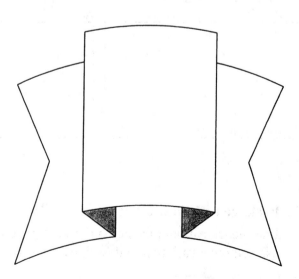

Power to Cure

Name_____   Date_____

Multiple Related Paragraphs

Prompt: You have been granted the power to cure or correct one malady of mankind.

Write three related paragraphs that address the criteria listed below:

Paragraph 1. Tell how you acquired the power to cure or correct a malady.

Paragraph 2. Tell what malady you have chosen to cure or correct.

Paragraph 3. Tell how it will affect life on the planet after you are finished.

You may also include other information relevant to your topic. Blend this information into your essay.

Examples:

1. How will the power work?

2. How long will the power last?

3. How long will it take to cure or correct the malady after you get started?

4. Do you have any personal connections to this story? If so, please include details.

Use the semantic organizer in the space below to plan the paragraphs.

1. Plot and Plan

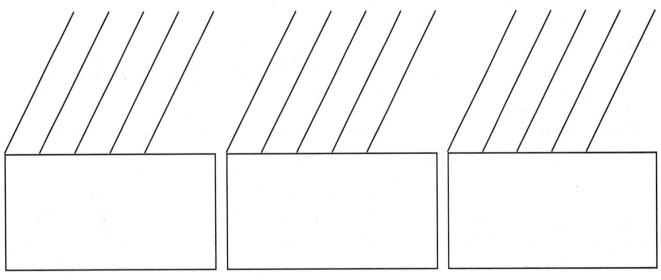

How I got the power   What I will cure   How it will affect life on Earth

2. Package and First Draft

Use the transitional frame on the next page to write the three related paragraphs. Remember to use sentence variety and descriptive words. Be creative and inventive.

Power to Cure *(cont.)*

Name_____   Date_____

Suddenly, I had the power in my own hands. It was the power to cure
_____. The circumstances were unusual. _____

_____

_____

_____

_____

_____

_____

_____

_____

I decided to use my power to cure _____ because

_____

_____

_____

_____

_____

_____

_____

_____

Having the power to cure _____ will affect all life on earth because

_____

_____

_____

_____

_____

_____

_____

Step 3: Prune and Plump   Step 4: Polish and Re-Write   Step 5: Publish and Perform

Introduction to Journaling

Daily Writing

Daily journal writing keeps students' writing skills sharp. Daily writing, like daily exercise, strengthens the hand muscles and makes the mechanical-physical task of writing easier. Daily writing emphasizes that writing should be part of everyday life. Daily writing conditions the student to silently verbalize thinking and put it into writing.

Writing Therapy

Students benefit from the opportunity to have a private journal because it provides them with the ability to verbalize feelings and emotions. Provide frequent opportunities for private journaling. This activity can come from a teacher prompt or from the student's need.

Private journals can be a part of the student's writing ring binder. Set the standard that no one opens another person's journal without permission. Pages that are folded back to the ring are for the owner's eyes only. If desired, the student can write permission for the teacher to read a passage on the front of the folded page.

Types of Journals

This book has a good selection of journal types. Teachers can print and hole-punch copies of new types of journaling activities at any time. It is convenient for students to add those to the journaling section of their ring binders. Provide daily writing journal pages at the beginning of the year and require students to write frequently.

All content areas fit well with journaling. Students who put thoughts into writing move up on the taxonomy of higher order thinking into application, analysis, synthesis, and evaluation. This improves learning in the content area.

Additional Journaling activities can include the following:

- response to literature or events
- information collection
- problem solving
- a break in a lesson
- assist comprehension
- debate
- reflect
- project log
- learning log
- on-going thematic dialog
- informal book report

- KWLs
- teacher information
- deep thinking
- self-analysis
- teacher-student dialog
- essay answers
- peer/pair interaction
- way to close or open lessons
- response to other students' work
- on-going communication with peer or tutor

Daily Journal

Name _____   Date _____

Monday	**Tuesday**
Wednesday	**Thursday**
Friday	**Weekend**

Journaling 1

Name_____   Date_____

Think about events and anticipate possible long-term effects of the events.

Think Deeply About Effects of an Event	
What happened?	**What could happen because of this?**

Journaling 2

Name_____ Date_____

Reflection

Describe the events.	How do I feel about the events?	What have I learned from this?

Journaling 3

Name_____   Date_____

Responsibility

Think about what you would like to know. How much do you already know? Make an initial (first) response. Later, think about these matters again, re-read your first response, and make a final judgment.

I Am Responsible for My Own Learning!		
I Know This	I Want to Know about This	I Have Learned This

Journaling 4

Name_____   Date_____

Response to Action

Think about events or actions that have taken place and make an initial (first) response. Later, think about the events again, re-read your first response, and make a final judgment.

Respond to Action		
Action What Happened?	My First Response!	After Thinking It Over, My Final Judgment

Journaling 5

Name_____   Date_____

Questioning Characters

Characters in a story have voices and motives (reasons) for their actions. Write about an imaginary interview with a character about motives, actions, and feelings. Write responses in the voice of the character.

Question Characters in a Story	
Interview Questions	**Character's Response**

Journaling 6

Name_____   Date_____

Reflect and Record

Personal Diary

Date_____

_____

_____

_____

_____

_____

Date_____

_____

_____

_____

_____

_____

Date_____

_____

_____

_____

_____

_____

Date_____

_____

_____

_____

_____

_____

Journaling

Journaling 7

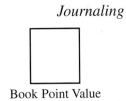

Book Point Value

Name_____   Date_____

Reading Journal

_____ Fiction   _____Title

_____ Nonfiction   _____Author

Write a summary of the book you read.

_____

_____

_____

_____

_____

Write a critique of the book. Make positive and negative comments.

Positive points about the book_____	Negative points about the book _____

Date _____

_____ Fiction   _____Title

_____ Nonfiction   _____Author

Write a summary of the book you read.

_____

_____

_____

_____

_____

Write a critique of the book. Make positive and negative comments

Positive points about the book_____	Negative points about the book _____

Journaling 8

Name_____ Date_____

Quotations to Remember

Most stories or lessons have information or passages that make you think deeply. In the spaces below, please re-write passages from stories or a lesson and tell what you thought after reading them.

Quotable Quotes and Puzzling Passages	
Rewrite the passage in the space below	Think about the passage and write a response

Journaling 9

Name_____   Date_____

Response to Literature

_____

Name of Story

Introduction to Writing Essays and Reports

Revise and Edit Checklist

Copy Revise and Edit Checklist (page 17) onto card stock. Cut into two sections. Three-hole punch the checklists and laminate for students. Students use this card as a reminder of the stages of writing and the writing attributes they are required to master. Also make multiple copies on plain paper and place them in a basket in the room. Students will use these to make notations.

Essays and Reports

This chapter is devoted to guiding students through writing essays and reports. After one or two models of guided essay and report writing, the teacher will understand the process and not have to labor over teacher instructions. For each new format, however, review the instructions. Subtle differences in each lesson are intended to make the student more independent.

In Chapter four, the teacher gradually kept less responsibility while the student assumed more responsibility for a writing assignment. At the end of the chapter, students started writing two and three related paragraphs with less and less guidance from the teacher. Writing two and three related paragraphs leads up to writing essays, reports, and in the next chapter, stories. The students become ready to think about how some ideas are related and yet can be developed independently as part of a larger project.

Like paragraphs, essays and reports need a beginning, middle, and ending. Different paragraphs can come together under a main idea to form essays, themes, stories, and reports. They flow together using transitional devices that lead the reader from one thought to the next.

Modeled Writing

Model the stages of developing an essay. Use timing strategies to keep students on the same task at the same time. When teaching guided writing for essays, do not assign the whole essay. Instead, model one stage at a time, following the formats provided in this chapter.

Make a transparency of the four-frame Modeled Five-Paragraph Plan on page 126.

Demonstrate that an essay starts with a single main idea. Point to the single box within frame 1.

Write "Three Wishes" in the top box of all four frames.

Point to box 2. Ask students to supply ideas for three wishes. Select three and write them in the three second level boxes of frames 2, 3, and 4.

Point to box 3. Tell students that each of the three wishes must have reasons or supporting details. For example, if students wished for a lot of money, ask them to supply ideas about how they would use a lot of money. Write those ideas on the small detail lines beneath the box.

Do the same for the other two boxes.

Tell students that the detail ideas transfer over to the fourth box. Point to frame 4 and the last box at the bottom of the frame. Tell students that it is the conclusion. Conclusions can do one of three things: summarize, re-state the main idea, or come to a new conclusion based on evidence presented in the middle.

Introduction to Writing Essays and Reports *(cont.)*

Modeled Writing *(cont.)*

Change the main idea and repeat the process using Essay and Report Organizers 1-a and 1-b (pages 127–128).

Print a transparency of Essay and Report Organizer 2-a (page 129). Organizers 2-b and 2-c (pages 130–131) are for your information. Use the plan to model a completed lesson. Let students hear you thinking aloud as you model each step, one step at a time.

Guided Writing

Print a transparency of A Bright Future blank (pages 132 and 133). A teacher example has been provided for you on pages 134 and 135. Follow the stages one at a time. The frame provides Step 1: Plot and Plan and Step 2: Package the First Draft. Use Revise and Edit Checklist to continue steps 3, 4, and 5.

Paper Folding Strategy

Read the instructions on Paper Folding Strategy (page 136). Paper folding strategy is a valuable concrete-to-abstract experience. Students learn with their hands, and the brain is able to attach an abstract thought to a concrete, physical experience.

Use paper folding strategy to guide students through the five-step writing process while completing the next assignment, Three Kind Deeds (page 137).

News Reporter (pages 138–140) emphasizes STAR Vocabulary. Distribute student copies and guide them through each stage.

Use timing and keep students together on the task. Once students start going ahead, others fall farther behind and the teacher winds up teaching on 25 different levels at once.

My Room (pages 141 and 142) has six webs and leads students to write seven paragraphs, followed by a transitional writing frame. For Unsung Heroes (pages 143 and 144), lead students to choose three subjects to write about, develop a STAR Vocabulary, and supply details about each person. Students follow the transitional writing frame to complete the essay. Use writing process steps 3, 4, and 5 to improve and correct the essay.

Follow instructions on individual lessons that follow in the chapter (pages 145–158).

Guide students as long as they need it. As students mature in a writing strategy, withdraw some of the support each time you do another version of that strategy.

> The writing goal for students is to analyze a prompt or assignment, determine what the end product should look like, and develop (or use an organizer to develop) the end product.
>
> Writing growth takes time and practice. Consistency is the best tool a teacher has.

Modeled Five-Paragraph Plan

The teacher can draw each step and add on during a demonstration of how to develop a beginning, middle, and ending, or duplicate this page on a transparency and show it on an overhead projector.

1. Beginning: introduce the main topic.

2. Middle: add three sub-topics.

3. Middle: plan details for each sub-topic.

4. Ending: plan a conclusion.

Essay and Report Organizer 1-a

Name _____

Date _____

Essay and Report Organizer 1-b

Name _____

Date _____

Essay and Report Organizer 2-a

Name_____   Date_____

Beginning

[ ]

_____

_____

_____

Middle

[| |]

_____   _____   _____
_____   _____   _____
_____   _____   _____
_____   _____   _____
_____   _____   _____
_____   _____   _____
_____   _____   _____

Ending

[ ]

Essay and Report Organizer 2-b

Name_____   Date_____

Beginning

> Write an attention-getting sentence.
>
> Write a main idea sentence including the three sub-topic ideas below.

Make a list of the three sub-topics

(a) _____

(b) _____

(c) _____

Middle

Write a sentence to introduce sub-topic (a).	Write a sentence to introduce sub-topic (b).	Write a sentence to introduce sub-topic (c).

List details for (a).   List details for (b).   List details for (c).

Ending

> Write a small paragraph for the ending. The ending can be a conclusion based on the evidence, a re-statement of the beginning paragraph using new words, or a brief summary of the entire essay.

Essay and Report Organizer 2-c

Name_____   Date_____

Beginning

Write an attention-getting sentence.

  Who ever heard of having a skunk for a pet?

Write a main idea sentence including the three sub-topic ideas below.

  As strange as it may sound, skunks and other unusual animals can make excellent pets. Just do not expect them to act like dogs and cats. My favorites were a pet skunk named Stinky, a hummingbird named Squeaky, and a duck named Puddles.

Make a list of the three sub-topics

  (a) *Stinky the skunk*

  (b) *Squeaky the hummingbird*

  (c) *Puddles the duck*

Middle

Write a sentence to introduce sub-topic (a).	Write a sentence to introduce sub-topic (b).	Write a sentence to introduce sub-topic (c).
First, Stinky the skunk came to my family when her mother was killed on the highway.	*Next, Squeaky joined our family one fall when he came inside our glass garden room and stayed.*	*Last, we hatched Puddles the duck from an egg. He thought I was his mother.*

List details for (a).	List details for (b).	List details for (c).
great watch "dog"	*fed him during the summer*	*science class project*
curious and funny	*may have been injured late in fall*	*last day of school*
great conversation starter	*became friendly*	*followed me around*
TV news team came	*I wore a bright red shirt*	*I took him home*
Stinky stayed until spring:	*sat on my shoulder*	*raised him in a box*
nature called and she left	*in spring went out*	*followed me all day*
		joined other ducks

Ending

Write a small paragraph for the ending. The ending can be a conclusion based on the evidence, a re-statement of the beginning paragraph using new words, or a brief summary of the entire essay.

Yes, some very unusual animals have been my favorite pets. They brought laughter to my life and opened my mind to a lifelong curiosity about animals and their behaviors. What I learned is that animals need love and care.

A Bright Future

Name_____   Date_____

> *Prompt:* Write a five paragraph essay that tells about three things you can do right now to assure your own bright future.

1. Plot and Plan

A. Plan the Beginning: Write an attention-getting sentence. (Example: I must take responsibility for my own future.) Change the prompt in the box above to make a thesis, or main idea statement. (Example: There are three things I can do now to assure I have a bright future.) Add a sentence that names the three things you can do now. (Example: I can stay in school, stay off drugs, and choose my friends wisely.) Write the two sentences in the box below.

| |
| |

B. Plan the Middle: Write sub-topic sentences in the three boxes below. Under the three boxes, make a list of related supporting details. On the next page, turn each detail item from the list into a sentence to create the three body paragraphs. Remember to use a variety of sentence styles and STAR Vocabulary

1.	2.	3.
First, I . . .	The second most important thing I can do is . . .	Additionally, I can . . .

list related details	*list related details*	*list related details*
_____	_____	_____
_____	_____	_____
_____	_____	_____
_____	_____	_____
_____	_____	_____

C. Plan the Conclusion

Restate the main idea from "A" again, re-affirming the statements and supporting statements. This can be very brief and should begin with transitional vocabulary that lets the reader know you are concluding your argument. (Example: In conclusion, my choices will determine my future. I will stay in school, stay off drugs, and choose my friends wisely.)

| |
| _____ |
| _____ |
| _____ |

2. Package the First Draft

A Bright Future *(cont.)*

Name_____   Date_____

(Transitional Word Frame)

    I must take responsibility for my own future. I can do many things now to assure that I will have a bright future. I believe that three of the most important to me are _____ , _____ , and _____ .

_____

_____

_____

    First, I _____

_____

_____

_____

_____

    The second most important thing I can do for myself to assure a bright future is to _____

_____

_____

_____

_____

    Additionally, I can _____

_____

_____

_____

_____

    In conclusion, my choices will _____

_____

_____

_____

_____

A Bright Future *(cont.)*

(Example of Teacher Modeled Lesson)

Name _____ Adam Green _____   Date _____ January 3 _____

1. Plot and Plan

  A. Plan the Beginning: Write an attention-getting sentence. (Example: I must take responsibility for my own future.) Turn the prompt into a thesis statement. (Example: There are three things I can do now to assure I have a bright future.) Add a sentence that names the three things you can do now. (Example: I can stay in school, stay off drugs, and choose my friends wisely.) Write the sentences in the box below.

> I must take responsibility for my own future. I can do at least three important things to assure that I have a bright future. Three things I can do are stay in school, stay off drugs, and choose my friends wisely.

  B. Plan the Middle: Write sub-topic sentences in the three boxes below. Under the three boxes, make a list of related supporting details. On the next page, turn each detail item from the list into a sentence to create the three body paragraphs. Remember to use a variety of sentence styles and STAR Vocabulary.

1.	2.	3.
First, I can stay in school	The second most important thing I can do is stay off drugs.	Additionally, I can choose my friends wisely, because friends influence thinking and behavior.

list related details	list related details	list related details
get good education	stay clear minded	surrounded by clean friends
study hard and succeed	stay healthy	safe friends environment
well-rounded in my thinking leads to successful career	clear police record	reputation of peers affects mine
I will provide for my future family	be a good example	friend networking offers

  C. Plan the Conclusion: Restate the main idea from "A" again, re-affirming the statements and supporting statements. This can be very brief and should begin with transitional vocabulary that lets the reader know you are concluding your argument. (Example: In conclusion, my choices will determine my future. I will stay in school, stay off drugs, and choose my friends wisely.

> I conclude that my future is largely up to me. My choices today influence my future. I will stay in school, stay away from illegal drugs, and choose my friends wisely. These three things will pave the way for a bright future for me.

A Bright Future *(cont.)*

(Example of Teacher-Modeled Lesson)

Name _____ Adam Green _____   Date _____ 1-3-06 _____

Transitional Word Frame

I can do many things to assure that I will have a bright future. I believe that three of the most important to me are **to stay in school , stay away from illegal drugs, and choose my friends wisely.**

First, I will **stay in school. I will study hard and do all my assignments. By doing this, I will surely succeed in school. Then, I can go to college and get a good education that will lead to a successful career. If I am successful in my career, I will be able to provide well for my future family. Having a good education will make me a well-rounded thinker who can make wise life decisions.**

The second most important thing I can do for myself to assure a bright future is to **stay off illegal drugs. My mind will stay clear, which will help with school. I will not engage in the risky behaviors drug addicts do, such as sharing needles. This will keep me healthy. People who use drugs do not think clearly. Sometimes they take chances with their safety, such as the way they drive a car. Staying away from illegal drugs will help assure my safety and help me make it to my future. I am sure I will never have a drug record with the police. I will be a good example of a "drug free teen" to my little brother. I will be helping others have a bright future by being an example.**

Additionally, I can **choose my friends wisely, because friends influence thinking and behavior. I will surround myself with friends who are clean of drugs, drinking, and alcohol. This will remove temptations. I will be a good example to them and they to me. A safe-friends environment will help both my friends and me to succeed in school and make good choices. The company I keep will reflect on me. Our individual reputations will affect each other. Friends who try hard are good resources. Parents and relatives of my friends may be the connection to finding good jobs or positions in the future. As they say, "It's who you know."**

In conclusion, **my choices today will influence my future. I will make conscious decisions that show I have my bright future in mind. I will stay in school and get a good, solid education so I will have a good career. I will stay off drugs so I can stay clear-minded, healthy, and safe. Choosing friends who have these same values will help me stay on track with my dreams of a bright future.**

Use Revise and Edit Checklist from page 17 to guide improvements to "A Bright Future."

3. Prune and Plump   **4. Polish and Re-Write**   **5. Publish and Perform**

Paper Folding Strategy

Concrete to Abstract: After students receive a prompt, teach paper-folding strategy to create a frame for essay or report writing. Start with a web organizer that uses the center for the main idea and uses three sub-topic circles with supporting details. Then fold the paper and draw columns and boxes. Write sentences in boxes according to the web.

Introductory Paragraph • Attention Getter • Main Idea Sentence (including the three sub-topic ideas)		
Introduce sub-topic 1	Introduce sub-topic 2	Introduce sub-topic 3
Supporting detail sentence for sub topic 1	Supporting detail sentence for sub topic 2	Supporting detail sentence for sub topic 3
Supporting detail sentence for sub topic 1	Supporting detail sentence for sub topic 2	Supporting detail sentence for sub topic 3
Supporting detail sentence for sub topic 1	Supporting detail sentence for sub topic 2	Supporting detail sentence for sub topic 3
Conclusion sentence or little incident supporting sub-topic 1	Conclusion sentence or little incident supporting sub-topic 2	Conclusion sentence or little incident supporting sub-topic 3
Conclusion for whole essay or report Conclusions can: • summarize • restate main idea • draw a conclusion based on the evidence		

Students start planning an essay by developing a graphic organizer for a writing assignment. Students fold paper down from the top and then up from the bottom. Next, students draw lines in the creases. Students draw vertical lines to create two to four columns in the middle, depending on the number of sub-topics. Students draw horizontal lines across to make sentence boxes. Students use the initial web graphic organizer and follow the pattern above to write an essay or report. This concrete-to-abstract experience remains with students. Even weak students learn this method and become successful in essay and report writing.

Three Kind Deeds

Name_____   Date_____

1. Plot and Plan: The plan has been made for you. Add your own details.

> Write an essay telling about the time you had to do three kind deeds before dark. Who or what required you to do the three kind deeds and why did you have to do them? Tell what three deeds you chose to do.
>
> In the middle, write a paragraph about each deed. Who benefited from the deed? Did the deed make a difference for someone else? If so, what? Conclude each middle paragraph with a little incident related to the good deeds.
>
> In conclusion, tell what you learned from the experience.

Fold a sheet of paper and draw the boxes like the pattern below.

Beginning Write an attention-getter. Who or what required you to do the deeds? Why did you have to do them? Name the deeds.			**Beginning**—*introductory paragraph*
Introduction to middle paragraph 1	Introduction to middle paragraph 2	Introduction to middle paragraph 3	**Middle**—*body paragraphs* Introduce each deed as a sub-topic paragraph. Use transitional words.
Detail-supporting sentence	Detail-supporting sentence	Detail-supporting sentence	Write detail sentences.
Detail-supporting sentence	Detail-supporting sentence	Detail-supporting sentence	Write detail sentences.
Detail-supporting sentence	Detail-supporting sentence	Detail-supporting sentence	Write detail sentences.
Little incident sentence	Little incident sentence	Little incident sentence	Conclude each paragraph. Consider writing about an incident telling what happened after the deed was done.
Write a conclusion. Choose one of these ideas: • Write a summary. • Re-state the introduction with different words. • Make a concluding statement based on the evidence you presented.			**Ending**—*conclusion paragraph*

2. Package the First Draft: Write the essay.

Use Revise and Edit Checklist as a guide through steps 3, 4 and 5.

3. Prune and Plump   **4. Polish and Re-Write**   **5. Publish and Perform**

News Reporter

Name_____   Date_____

1. Plot and Plan

A. Ask the local newspaper to donate enough same-copy newspapers for the whole class.

B. Study the list of types of newspaper articles below. Hold class or smal-group discussions about any unfamiliar types of articles. Skim the newspaper and try to identify the types of articles you find. Read articles of interest. Notice the features of different newspaper types.

Types of Articles in Newspapers and Magazines

• book reviews	• feature	• how-to	• local news
• movie reviews	• food	• humor	• medical
• business	• gardening	• informational	• opinion
• editorials	• general interest	• inspirational	• politics
• fashion	• historical	• interview	• sports

C. Choose one type of newspaper article from the list above. Skim and read the newspaper, looking for a sample of the type of article you have chosen. You are to write a newspaper article of that type. Clip out a sample newspaper article for reference.

D. Write the type of news article you have chosen in the box below.

E. Use STAR Vocabulary words from the list below; add your own words to the list. Hold a class or small-group discussion about any unfamiliar words and their meanings.

• accuracy	• edition	• lead paragraph	_____
• advertising	• editor	• lead story	
• anecdotes	• editorial	• news story	_____
• angle	• editor-in-chief	• nonfiction	
• audience	• entertainment	• opinion	_____
• breaking story	• facts	• photo essay	
• cartoons	• feature story	• press release	_____
• column	• free lance	• quote	
• cover story	• headline	• reporter	_____
• dateline	• human interest		
• deadline	• investigation	_____	_____

Notes: _____

_____

_____

News Reporter *(cont.)*

F. Write a boldface attention-getting headline using two to six words.

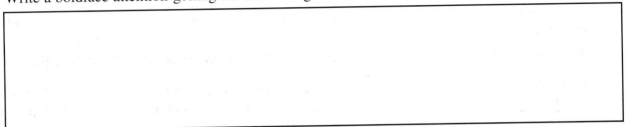

G. In the wheel below, collect information about the article you have chosen to write.

H. Put the information in order below. Put the most important information first, followed by related details, data, or human interest information.

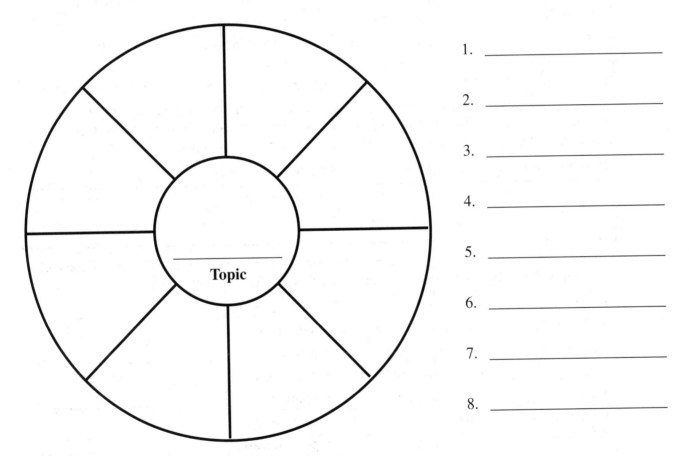

Topic

1. _____

2. _____

3. _____

4. _____

5. _____

6. _____

7. _____

8. _____

I. Study the lead paragraph of the sample article you clipped. The lead paragraph must hook and hold the reader. It must be interesting and get right to the main idea of the article. Hold a class or small group discussion about the strengths of the lead paragraphs of the sample articles.

_____

_____

News Reporter *(cont.)*

2. Package the First Draft

Write the first draft of the article using column form found in a newspaper articles. Remember, all writing needs a beginning, middle, and an ending. Write a lead paragraph that hooks and holds the reader. Write sentences or paragraphs about each idea from list H above. Put the most important information first. Write a conclusion.

3. Prune and Plump: Ask a peer or teacher to help you find needed revisions. Over-write with a different colored pen or erase and re-write. Improve sentences with description.

4. Polish and Re-Write a final draft: Ask a peer to help you make final changes in spelling, capitalization, punctuation, or other needed changes.

5. Publish and Perform: Print your article in the school newspaper or read aloud.

My Room

Name_____   Date_____

Collect information on each web about the things you notice in your room. Add more lines if needed. Use the webs to write information on the following transitional frame.

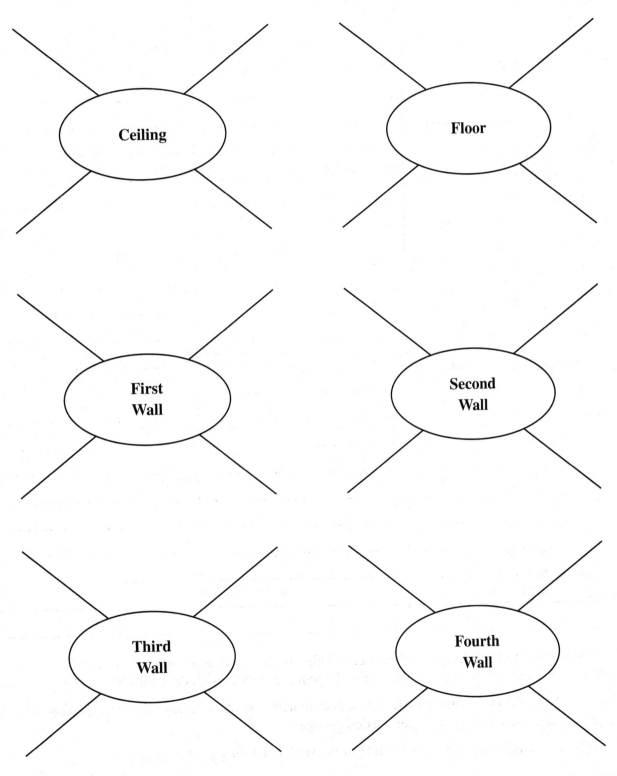

My Room *(cont.)*

Name _____   Date _____

Suddenly, without warning, I was confined to my room. _____

_____

_____

_____

Out of sheer boredom, I started looking around. To my amazement, I started to see things _____

_____

_____

_____

That prompted me to look closely at all the details in the room. I looked toward _____

_____

_____

_____

To my right, I noticed _____

_____

_____

_____

The wall to my left _____

_____

_____

_____

I was forced to look behind me just to see things I had never noticed before. I saw _____

_____

_____

_____

Pure curiosity caused me to look up at the ceiling, probably for the first time in my life. _____

_____

_____

_____

Finally, just to put closure to the curiosity of my brain, I peered over the edge of the bed and saw

_____

_____

_____

Unsung Heroes

Name _____   Date _____

1. Plot and Plan

Heroes are all around you. Think of three people you admire: one family member, one friend, and one person from the community. Write their names in the centers of the webs below. Write words on the lines that represent the personality traits of each one. Write a paragraph about each one. Develop STAR Vocabulary in the blanks below for use in the essay.

Sensory	**Technical**	**Articulate**	**Realistic**
_____	_____	_____	_____
_____	_____	_____	_____
_____	_____	_____	_____

(1)   (2)   (3)

2. Package the First Draft

My Three Heroes

   Not all heroes get the recognition they deserve. They are the heroes who live among us and no one pays attention to their great qualities. I think they need some recognition. _____ , _____ and _____ , are unsung heroes. They are people I really know.

   First, I chose to name _____ as an unsung hero because _____

_____

_____

_____

_____

_____

_____

_____

_____

_____

_____

_____

Unsung Heroes (cont.)

My Three Heroes (cont.)

Second, I call _____ an unsung hero because _____

_____

_____

_____

_____

_____

_____

The third unsung hero I know is _____ . This person _____

_____

_____

_____

_____

_____

_____

_____

In conclusion, the people I named and the qualities they possess inspire me to _____

_____

_____

_____

_____

_____

_____

_____

3. Prune and Plump   **4. Polish and Re-Write**   **5. Publish and Perform**

Communication

(Featuring STAR Vocabulary!)

			Add your own vocabulary in the blanks. Include jargon you and your friends use to communicate.
AM	letter	radar	
answer	letter carrier	radio	
arrival	mail	regulations	_____
bands	mail train	satellite	
cable	modem	signal	
cellular	On-Star	telephone	_____
communicate	package	telegraph	
computer	parcel	television	
e-business	pony express	train	_____
e-mail	portable	UPS	
electronic	portable phone	wireless	_____
FM	postal	You've got mail!	
in-box	post office	snail mail	_____
Internet	phone		

1. Plot and Plan

Use STAR Vocabulary from the lists above in a report on communications in the modern world compared to communication one hundred years ago. Discuss the things that are still the same. You will have to do some research. Organize information on the Venn diagram below. Write the report on your own paper or use word processing. The report needs an introduction, a body, and a conclusion.

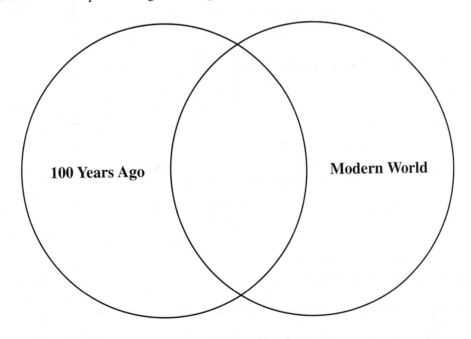

100 Years Ago   **Modern World**

2. Package the First Draft
3. Prune and Plump   ## 4. Polish and Re-Write   ## 5. Publish and Perform

Time and Ages

adolescence	decade	obsolete	sunset
adulthood	immature	old	teenage
age	infancy	old age	worn-out
ancient	late	outdated	young
baby	mature	overdue	youth
babyhood	middle age	prehistoric	_____
century	minute	slowly	_____
childhood	modern	speedy	_____
crawling	new	sunrise	

Write a poetic essay that ponders and reflects on the times and ages of a lifespan. Use vocabulary from the list above and use a thesaurus to find synonyms or antonyms for those words. Think about what your grandmother or grandfather might say about how quickly time passes. Think about what a life should represent once it is finished.

Organize your thinking by writing notes on the frame below. Write a first draft, edit, and write a final draft on your own paper or use computer word processing.

Introduction:			
Babyhood	**Childhood**	**Adulthood**	**Old Age**
Conclusion:			

(Write on the back if necessary.)

Jazzy Transportation

(Featuring STAR Vocabulary!)

blow	roar	*Add vocabulary words of your own.*	
blow the horn	roared		
careened	shiny	_____	_____
chrome	skidded	_____	_____
communicate	sleek	_____	_____
converse	slid	_____	_____
conversation	shot ahead	_____	_____
crash	souped-up	_____	_____
curve	speed	_____	_____
fast	steer	_____	_____
fender	tires	_____	_____
fender bender	tires screaming	_____	_____
metallic	train	_____	_____
metallic paint	velvety	_____	_____
move	veered	_____	_____
paint job	zoom	_____	_____
paint stripes		_____	_____
pass		_____	_____
passed		_____	_____
passing zone		_____	_____

Write an essay about transportation using the five-step writing process you have learned. Discuss the transportation you have, the transportation you would like to have, and transportation as you imagine it in the future. The sky is not the limit. Use your imagination. Use the graphic organizer below to plan the essay. Write on your own paper or use computer word processing. Use STAR Vocabulary in the essay.

Introduction	**Transportation I have:**	**Conclusion**
	Transportation I would like to have:	
	Transportation as I imagine it in the future:	

Food

(Featuring STAR Vocabulary!)

appealing	delightful	mash	savory
appetizer	doughnut	mashed	scaly
appetite	dip	meat	scrumptious
apple	easy	meaty	sharp
awful	fizzy	mild	slurpy
banana	food	moist	smooth
batter	freezing	mush	snap beans
bread	fresh	mushy	sour
bitter	frosty	jar	succulent
bright	fruity	jazz	spicy
brittle	gooey	orange	steaming
butter	green	peas	steamy
cantaloupe	guava	pepper	sticky
chewy	healthy	peppery	sticky bun
chips	hearty	popcorn	sweet
chunky	hot	popping	tangy
cold	ice	potatoes	tart
cool	icy	pumpernickel	tasty
colorful	ice cream	raw	tea
creamy	icicle	red	tender
crisp	ice pop	Reuben	thick
crumbly	ice sculpture	rich	toasted
crunchy	image	ripe	yellow
crusty	juicy	round	warm
curly	jam	runny	wet
delicate	leafy	rye	wrinkled
delicious	lean	salty	

Use the five-step writing process for this assignment. Use vocabulary from the above list. Add other related vocabulary to the list. Create an advertisement campaign for a specialty restaurant in town. Draw a plan for a highway billboard below. Write a song or jingle for the advertisements. Write the words for a television commercial. Use your own paper or use computer word processing.

How to _____

Name_____   Date_____

1. **Plot and Plan:** Use the organizer below to guide you in writing instructions on how to do something. Examples: how to make a sandwich, bake cookies, grow flowers, sew on a button. Use more than one page if necessary. Draw pictures before writing.

Materials   **Tools**

_____   _____

_____   _____

_____   _____

_____   _____

_____   _____

_____   _____

Step | I | 2. **Package the First Draft**

Illustration   Written Instructions

How to _____ *(cont.)*

Step ☐

Illustration   Written Instructions

Step ☐

Illustration   Written Instructions

(Make additional copies for extra steps.)

3. Prune and Plump   **4. Polish and Re-Write**   **5. Publish and Perform**

Framework to Show Change

Name_____   Date_____

1. Plot and Plan

Use this sequence frame to plan an essay dealing with change. Example topics include a seed growing into a plant; a baby changing as it grows; seasons; scenery on a vacation; historical events; or a character changing such as Buck, the dog in the story *Call of the Wild* by Jack London.

Describe the beginning.

Beginning

Event causing change

Event causing change

Event causing change

Event causing change

Describe the ending.

End

Framework to Show Change *(cont.)*

Name_____   Date_____

2. Package the First Draft

Directions: Write a paragraph about each stage of change from the planner on page 151. You will need two copies of this page for eight paragraphs.

_____

_____

_____

_____

_____

_____

_____

_____

_____

_____

_____

_____

_____

_____

_____

_____

_____

_____

_____

_____

_____

_____

_____

_____

_____

3. Prune and Plump   **4. Polish and Re-Write**   **5. Publish and Perform**

The Five-Paragraph Essay

(Essay Frame: 5 Ws)

Name _____   Date _____

Beginning: Start with an attention-getting device. The introductory sentence tells the main topic of the essay and names the three sub-topics. TR = use a transitional word. ¶ = indent for a new paragraph.		
Middle: Body paragraphs begin with a Who or What sentence. The next two boxes will tell When, Where, How, or Why. The last sentence of each paragraph is an example or incident sentence.		
¶ Who or What is the subject?	¶ Who or What is the subject?	¶ Who or What is the subject?
When, Where, How, or Why	When, Where, How, or Why	When, Where, How, or Why
When, Where, How, or Why	When, Where, How, or Why	When, Where, How, or Why
Example or Incident (little story)	Example or Incident (little story)	Example or Incident (little story)
Ending: The conclusion paragraph (1) summarizes, (2) re-states the main topic, or (3) comes to a conclusion based on the evidence presented. The concluding paragraph lets the reader know the essay is finished.		
¶		

Generic Essay Writing Frame

Name_____   Date_____

Introductory Paragraph

(Introduces the topic and sub-topic ideas—minimum 50 words.)

_____

_____

_____

_____

_____

_____

_____

_____

_____

_____

_____

Body

(Body paragraph one gives details about the first sub-topic—minimum 75 words.)

_____

_____

_____

_____

_____

_____

_____

_____

_____

_____

_____

_____

_____

_____

Generic Essay Writing Frame (cont.)

Name_____   Date_____

Body *(cont.)*
(Body paragraph two gives details about the second sub-topic—minimum 75 words.)

_____

_____

_____

_____

_____

_____

(Body paragraph three gives details about the third sub-topic—minimum 75 words.)

_____

_____

_____

_____

_____

_____

Conclusion
(The conclusion summarizes the ideas of the essay or draws a conclusion point based on the
information presented within the essay—minimum 30 words.)

_____

_____

_____

_____

_____

Time Capsule

_____

Year Buried

My name is _____. I am _____.

_____

_____

What I want to remember about the _____ school year is _____.

_____

_____

My closest friends are _____.

_____

_____

We _____

_____

My teachers are _____, and _____,

_____, _____,

_____, _____,

_____, _____,

_____, _____, and

_____, _____.

My favorite subject is _____ because _____.

_____

_____.

Time Capsule *(cont.)*

I plan to become a/an _____

because _____.

My favorite song is _____.

My favorite hobby is _____.

My room at home is _____.

_____

_____

The things that bug me most are _____.

_____

_____

I think that my best gifts or talents are _____.

_____

_____

I would describe myself as _____.

_____

_____

When I am 50, I want to look back on my life and say I accomplished _____

_____

_____.

Sunburst Essay Planner

Name_____   Date_____

1. Plot and Plan

Directions: Remember the five-step planner you learned? Here is a different format using the same ideas. Use it to write an essay expressing your opinion about a topic. Sample topics:

- Why School Should Not Start Early in the Morning
- Why Teens Should Have Privacy
- Why College Should Be Free to Everyone

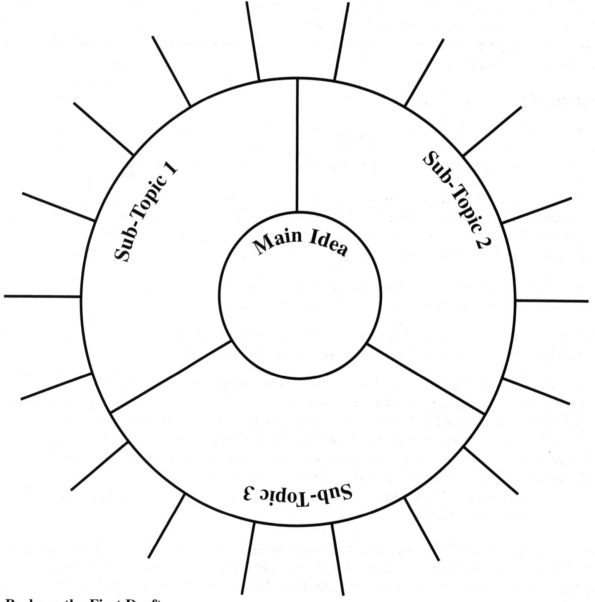

2. Package the First Draft

Use Generic Essay Writing Frame (pages 154 and 155) to write the essay or use your own paper. Follow steps 3, 4, and 5 to finish the writing process.

3. Prune and Plump   ## 4. Polish and Re-Write   ## 5. Publish and Perform

Introduction to Story Writing

Planning

In the chapters on sentence building, paragraph writing, journaling, and essay writing, students have practiced writing as a process. A well-planned process yields a good product. Planning is the single most important part of the writing process. Good planning includes visualizing the final product and creating an organizer to develop that final product. Good planning eliminates most writing problems before they happen.

Bring the Story to Life

This chapter introduces a variety of organizers for helping students develop a good story plan. Once the story plan is in place, teach students to start imagining the characters' speech and actions. Illustrate the process by bringing in some toy action figures. Ask two or three students to use the figures to act out the story and speak the dialog.

Beginning, Middle, Ending

Like all good writing, story writing has a beginning, middle, and ending. Stories also have characters, setting, problem, and solution. Always introduce characters, setting, and the story problem in the beginning of a story. Once these elements are in place, the middle of the story begins.

1. *The most important element of a story is the problem.* The problem is the engine of a story. Students must develop logical, believable problems. Sometimes students will say the problem is "Josh died." If Josh is the main character and he dies in the beginning, where the problem is, then the story may be over before it begins.

2. For a writing selection to be considered a story, it must have a beginning, middle, and ending. The beginning must contain the characters, setting, and introduce the problem.

3. *Next, it is imperative to guide students to plan the ending before they plan the middle.* Students must have the end in mind when they develop events in the middle.

4. *Develop the middle events and adventures last.* If the writer has the end in mind, it acts as a writing road map. The writer then can visualize what events could logically happen in the middle. The characters try to solve the story problem during the middle of the story. Basic three-event stories have the characters dedicated to solving the story problem. (Longer stories can digress a bit, go into detail about scenery and peripheral events, but the problem still looms over the characters.) Student writing is generally the first type. In the beginning, weave in the characters, setting, and problem. The characters immediately set about trying to solve the problem. These are the events of the middle.

Eventually, the characters find a plan that works—the solution. Once the solution is reached, the story is basically over. Because of the problem, however, something changes in the lives of the characters. The epilog is what happens to the characters after the solution. Characters or situations are basically changed forever.

Introduction to Story Writing *(cont.)*

Prompts

A story prompt is a story problem. Develop a story prompt list. Everyday occurrences are good story prompts. Students may tend to write about interpersonal relationships between friends. Broaden their thinking by challenging them with higher-order problems if possible.

Steps to Good Story Writing

1. Plot and Plan

   a. Research background information and develop a STAR Vocabulary. This will make the story realistic.

   b. Choose a plan. This book contains many good story planners. Simply insert the problem into the slot, develop or import characters, plan how the problem will be solved, and then plan events that logically fit in the middle. Always use that sequence.

      Story prompts can supply the problem. Story prompts seldom supply events for the middle or a solution for the ending.

      This book teaches students to develop a Trademark Character and his family and friends. The Trademark Character can be inserted into almost any story. The rules for Trademark Characters are these: the character *cannot change personalities in different stories;* the character *cannot be killed off;* the character *should have some redeeming qualities.*

      Always look over a student's story plan or have it briefly read aloud. Give immediate feedback. Learn strategies for correcting and giving positive feedback at the same time. Negative feedback can stop students from writing—forever! Field trials of this text have revealed that even learning disabled students can use the support systems supplied in this text, master them, and become able to plan independently.

2. Package the First Draft

   a. Tell students to imagine the characters talking and their actions. To hook the reader, teach students to start off with action, noise, dialog, an argument, or something attention-grabbing.

   b. The story planner is not the story. It can be a rough draft or a summary draft. Story planners are designed to help the student see the "big picture" before starting to write.

   c. Students use STAR Vocabulary as a valuable tool for developing exciting stories.

   d. It is essential for students to be satisfied with the original story plan before they write the first draft. Major changes will have a domino effect on the elements of the story.

Introduction to Story Writing *(cont.)*

Steps to Good Story Writing *(cont.)*

3. Prune and Plump

After writing a first draft, students seldom are able to immediately see any errors. The mind is in a different phase by then and does not register what is really there. It registers what it planned for the hand to write. The hand works considerably slower than the mind, so many pieces of valuable information may have been skipped. The paper needs to become "cold" before the student can see any errors. Give students the red pen and ask them to self-correct by over-writing on top of the original. Students may choose to erase and re-write. Word processing allows students to delete and move text.

Students should take out any part of the story that does not connect. Frequently students need to fill in gaps in transition or information.

Position yourself where you can both see all students and also begin short one-minute conferences with students. Establish a pattern of conferencing order or you will find yourself surrounded by students waiting for a conference. Sign-up sheets work well. Students sign up when they are nearly finished. That way you are conferencing with the ones who are finished while the ones who are not continue working. Typically, once the routine is established, the flow becomes good. Over-writing or erasing and re-writing save students from many drafts.

Trick: Change forms or colors for each draft you require. Examples: STAR Vocabulary is green, Story Planner is pink, and first draft is yellow. Final draft is white. Students easily accept that the story will be written or planned over the period of four colors of paper.

4. Polish and Re-Write

After a conference, students write or word process a final draft. The final draft should have a presentable, neat appearance. To help students with their revisions and editing, use the Revise and Edit Checklist (page 17) after adding these Story Elements to the bottom of the list:

Story Elements

____well-developed characters

____vivid description of setting

____clearly defined problem

____problem and solution well-connected

____logical/reasonable solution

5. Publish and Perform

Students enjoy celebrating their accomplishments. Display papers with construction paper backgrounds, geometric cutouts, or other dramatic looks. Plan parent nights for students to read their works aloud. Publish stories in the school newspaper. Conduct competitions and announce winners. Help students enter contests conducted by outside organizations.

Story Re-Telling A

Name_____   Date_____

> **Assignment:** You will read or listen to a story. Your teacher will guide you step by step in re-telling the beginning, middle, and ending of the story. Do not work ahead without teacher permission.

Beginning of the Story: The writer always introduces main characters, setting, and the story problem. Secondary characters can enter the story in the middle or ending, but a good writer plans those characters in advance. Setting describes where the story takes place. Setting also includes time. Time can be vague or specific: century, year, season, day, hour, or minute. In a story, characters always have a problem to solve.

Main Character: Name and write a description of the main character.	**Secondary Character:** Name and write a description of a secondary character.
Setting: Write a description, including time and place.	**Problem:** In a story, characters have a problem to solve. Clearly describe the problem.

Middle of the Story: Write about three events or adventures that happen in the middle while the characters are trying to solve the problem. Do not write about the solution.

Event 1:	Event 2:	Event 3:

Ending of the Story: The ending has a solution and an epilog.

Solution: Write about how the characters solve the problem.	**Epilog:** Write about what happens last.

Story Planner A

Name_____   Date_____

Assignment: Use what you learned from Story Re-Telling A to design your own story. Your teacher will guide you step by step. Do not work ahead of the class.

1. **Plot and Plan**
2. **Package the First Draft**

Beginning of the Story: The writer always introduces main characters, setting, and the story problem. Secondary characters can enter the story in the middle or ending, but a good writer plans those characters in advance. Setting describes where the story takes place. Setting also includes time. Time can be vague or specific: century, year, season, day, hour, or minute. In a story, characters always have a problem to solve.

Main Character: Name and write a description of the main character.	**Secondary Character:** Name and write a description of a secondary character.
Setting: Write a description, including time and place.	**Problem:** In a story, characters have a problem to solve. Clearly describe the problem.

Middle of the Story: Write about three events or adventures that happen in the middle while the characters are trying to solve the problem. Do not write about the solution.

Event 1:	**Event 2:**	**Event 3:**

Ending of the Story: The ending has a solution and an epilog.

Solution: Write about how the characters solve the problem.	**Epilog:** Write about what happens last.

Story Re-Telling B

Name_____   Date_____

> **Assignment:** You will read or listen to a story. Your teacher will guide you step by step in re-telling the beginning, middle, and ending of the story. Do not work ahead without teacher permission.

Beginning: The writer always introduces main characters, setting, and the story problem in the beginning. Secondary characters can enter the story in the middle or ending, but a good writer plans those characters in advance. Setting describes where the story takes place. Setting also includes time. Time can be vague or specific: century, year, season, day, hour, or minute. In a story, characters always have a problem to solve. Write whole-sentence answers.

1. Name and describe the main character. _____

   _____

2. Name and describe a secondary character. _____

   _____

3. Describe the setting, including time and place. _____

   _____

4. Describe the problem of the story. _____

   _____

Middle: Write about the events or adventures that happen in the middle of the story while the characters are trying to solve the problem. Do not write about the solution.

Adventure 1: _____

_____

_____

Adventure 2: _____

_____

_____

Adventure 3: _____

_____

_____

Ending: The ending of a story has a solution and an epilog. Write about how the characters solve the problem. **Epilog:** after the problem is solved, what happens to everyone in the story? How is the story ending different from the beginning? _____

_____

_____

Story Planner B

Name_____   Date_____

Assignment: Use what you learned about re-telling a story from the previous lesson. Your teacher will guide you step by step in designing a beginning, middle, and ending of a story. Do not work ahead without teacher permission.

---

1. Plot and Plan   **2. Package the First Draft**

Beginning: The writer always introduces main characters, setting, and the story problem in the beginning. Secondary characters can enter the story in the middle or ending, but a good writer plans those characters in advance. Setting describes where the story takes place. Setting also includes time. Time can be vague or specific: century, year, season, day, hour, or minute. In a story, characters always have a problem to solve. Write whole-sentence answers.

1. Name and describe the main character. _____

_____

_____

2. Name and describe a secondary character. _____

_____

_____

3. Describe the setting, including time and place. _____

_____

_____

4. Describe the problem of the story. _____

_____

_____

Middle: Write about the events or adventures that happen in the middle of the story while the characters are trying to solve the problem. Do not write about the solution.

Adventure 1: _____

_____

Adventure 2: _____

_____

Adventure 3: _____

_____

Ending: The ending of a story has a solution and an epilog. Write about how the characters solve the problem. Epilog: after the problem is solved, what happens to everyone in the story? How is the story ending different from the beginning?

_____

_____

---

3. Prune and Plump   **4. Polish and Re-Write**   **5. Publish and Perform**

Generic Story Writing Frame 1

Name_____   Date_____

Story Title

Beginning: The beginning of a story introduces characters, setting, and the story problem. The beginning must "hook" the reader.

_____

_____

_____

_____

_____

_____

_____

_____

_____

_____

_____

_____

Middle: The characters continue to try to solve the story problem but cannot until the ending of the story. In the meantime, they have adventures and misadventures while trying to solve the problem. Write about three of the adventures.

Adventure 1

_____

_____

_____

_____

_____

_____

_____

_____

_____

_____

_____

Generic Story Writing Frame 1 (cont.)

Adventure 2

_____

_____

_____

_____

_____

_____

_____

_____

Adventure 3

_____

_____

_____

_____

_____

_____

_____

_____

Ending

_____

_____

_____

_____

_____

_____

_____

_____

Story Re-Telling C

Name _____

Date _____

Directions: Listen to or read a story and re-tell the story using the story frame below.

Write STAR Vocabulary in this box.

1. **Plot and Plan**
2. **Package First Draft**

Title of Story _____

Beginning	Middle	Ending
Problem	Event 1	Solution
Characters	Event 2	
Setting	Event 3	Changes (at end of story)
time _____		
season _____		
place _____		

3. **Prune and Plump**   4. **Polish and Re-Write**   5. **Publish and Perform**

Story Planner C

Name _____   Date _____

Directions: Use what you learned from Story Re-telling C to plan a story. The teacher will assign a prompt and guide you while you develop a story plan.

Write STAR Vocabulary in this box.

1. **Plot and Plan**
2. **Package First Draft**

Title of Story _____

Beginning	Middle	Ending
Problem	**Event 1**	**Solution**
Characters	**Event 2**	
Setting	**Event 3**	**Changes** (at end of story)
time _____		
season _____		
place _____		

3. **Prune and Plump**   4. **Polish and Re-Write**   5. **Publish and Perform**

Story Re-telling D

Name _____   Date _____

1. Plot and Plan   2. Package the First Draft

Listen to or read a story. Re-tell the story on the frame below.
Draw a scene from the story in the space to the right. Fill in
the information on the lines to the bottom right of the page.

Beginning of Story

Middle of Story

Ending of Story

Characters

_____

_____

_____

_____

Setting

_____

_____

_____

_____

Problem

_____

_____

_____

_____

Solution

_____

_____

_____

_____

STAR Vocabulary

_____

_____

_____

_____

3. Prune and Plump   4. Polish and Re-Write   5. Publish and Perform

Story Planner D: Sports Story

Name_____   Date_____

1. Plot and Plan   **2. Package the First Draft**

Design a story that has a beginning, middle, and ending. Draw a scene from the story in the upper right side of the page. Plan the characters, setting, problem, solution, and STAR Vocabulary in the lower right hand spaces. Write a summary first draft in the space below.

Beginning of Story

Middle of Story

Ending of Story

Characters

_____
_____
_____

Setting

_____
_____
_____

Problem

_____
_____
_____

Solution

_____
_____
_____

STAR Vocabulary

_____
_____
_____

3. Prune and Plump   **4. Polish and Re-Write**   **5. Publish and Perform**

Generic Story Writing Frame 2

1. **Plot and Plan**
2. **Package the First Draft**

Story Title

Beginning

_____
_____
_____
_____
_____
_____
_____
_____
_____
_____

_____
_____
_____
_____
_____
_____
_____
_____
_____
_____

Ending

Middle

_____
_____
_____
_____
_____
_____
_____
_____
_____
_____
_____
_____
_____
_____

_____
_____
_____
_____
_____
_____
_____
_____
_____

3. **Prune and Plump**
4. **Polish and Re-write**
5. **Publish and Perform**

Story Planner D: **Animal**

Name _____   Date _____

1. Plot and Plan   **2. Package the First Draft**

Design a story that has a beginning, middle, and ending.
Draw a scene from the story in the upper right side of the
page. Plan the characters, setting, problem, solution, and
STAR Vocabulary in the lower right hand spaces. Write a
summary first draft in the space below.

Beginning of Story

Middle of Story

Ending of Story

Characters

_____
_____
_____

Setting

_____
_____
_____

Problem

_____
_____
_____

Solution

_____
_____
_____

STAR Vocabulary

_____
_____
_____

3. Prune and Plump   **4. Polish and Re-Write**   **5. Publish and Perform**

Generic Story Writing Frame 3

Name _____

Date _____

1. **Plot and Plan**
2. **Package the First Draft**
   Create a story planner of your own and write the first draft on this page.

Title of Story _____

Beginning	Middle	Ending

3. **Prune and Plump**   4. **Polish and Re-Write**   5. **Publish and Perform**

Story Planner D: Pirate

Name_____   Date_____

1. Plot and Plan   2. Package the First Draft

Design a story that has a beginning, middle, and ending. Draw a scene from the story in the upper right side of the page. Plan the characters, setting, problem, solution, and STAR Vocabulary in the lower right hand spaces. Write a summary first draft in the space below.

Beginning of Story

Middle of Story

Ending of Story

Characters

_____
_____
_____

Setting

_____
_____
_____

Problem

_____
_____
_____

Solution

_____
_____
_____

STAR Vocabulary

_____
_____
_____

3. Prune and Plump   4. Polish and Re-Write   5. Publish and Perform

Story Planner D: NASA

Name_____

Date_____

1. Plot and Plan

2. Package the First Draft

Design a story that has a beginning, middle, and ending. Draw a scene from the story in the upper right side of the page. Plan the characters, setting, problem, solution, and STAR Vocabulary in the lower right hand spaces. Write a summary first draft in the space below.

Beginning of Story

Middle of Story

Ending of Story

Characters

_____
_____
_____
_____

Setting

_____
_____
_____

Problem

_____
_____
_____

Solution

_____
_____
_____

STAR Vocabulary

_____
_____
_____
_____

3. Prune and Plump

4. Polish and Re-Write

5. Publish and Perform

Story Planner D

Name_____   Date_____

Title

1. Plot and Plan   2. Package the First Draft

Design a story that has a beginning, middle, and ending. Draw a scene from the story in the upper right side of the page. Plan the characters, setting, problem, solution, and STAR Vocabulary in the lower right hand spaces. Write a summary first draft in the space below.

Beginning of Story

Middle of Story

Ending of Story

Characters

_____

_____

_____

_____

Setting

_____

_____

_____

Problem

_____

_____

_____

Solution

_____

_____

_____

_____

STAR Vocabulary

_____

_____

_____

_____

3. Prune and Plump   4. Polish and Re-Write   5. Publish and Perform

Story Planner E: Visualizer

Name_____   Date_____

Directions: Select a story topic. Plan the story by drawing it first. Follow the plan below. Use a STAR Vocabulary sheet to develop a stellar vocabulary.

1. **Plot and Plan:** The beginning of a story contains characters, setting, and problem.

Story Beginning: Draw and label the characters.

Draw and label a picture of the setting.

Draw and label a picture of the problem. Use speech bubbles to tell words of characters.

Story Planner E: Visualizer *(cont.)*

Name_____   Date_____

1. Plot and Plan *(cont.)*

Story Middle: A story middle contains the adventures and misadventures of the characters as they try to solve the problem.

Draw and label the events, adventures, and misadventures along the way. Use speech bubbles to show what the characters are saying.

1.

2.

3.

Story Ending: The story ending contains the solution to the problem and an epilog.

Solution

Epilog

2. Package the First Draft: Write on a writing frame or your own paper.   3. Prune and Plum.

4. Polish and Re-Write: Use word processing or write a neat copy.   5. Publish and Perform

Story Planner F: Journey into Space

1. Plot and Plan

Directions: Develop a space-related STAR Vocabulary list and create a story plot including characters, setting, problem, and solution.

2. Package the First Draft

Beginning	Middle	Ending
Characters	Adventure 1	Solution
Setting	Adventure 2	
Problem	Adventure 3	Epilog
STAR Vocabulary		

3. Prune and Plump   4. Polish and Re-Write   5. Publish and Perform

Generic Story Writing Frame 4

1. **Plot and Plan**
2. **Package the First Draft**

Story Title _____

Beginning

_____
_____
_____
_____
_____
_____
_____
_____
_____
_____
_____
_____

Middle

_____
_____
_____
_____
_____
_____
_____
_____
_____
_____
_____
_____

Ending

_____
_____
_____
_____
_____
_____
_____

3. **Prune and Plump**
4. **Polish and Re-Write**
5. **Publish and Perform**

Story Planner F: The Big Test

1. Plot and Plan

Directions: Develop a STAR Vocabulary list and create a story plot about a big test including characters, setting, problem, and solution.

2. Package the First Draft (Write in tne boxes below.)

Beginning

Characters	
Setting	
Problem	
STAR Vocabulary	

Middle

Adventure 1
Adventure 2
Adventure 3

Ending

Solution
Epilog

3. Prune and Plump (Erase or overwrite to revise the story.)

4. Polish and Re-Write (Write on your own paper.)

5. Publish and Perform

Story Planner F: The Day the Relatives Came

1. Plot and Plan   **2. Package the First Draft** (Write in the boxes below.)

Directions: Create a humorous story plot about the day relatives came to visit. Develop a STAR Vocabulary list.

Beginning

Characters

Setting

Problem

Middle

Adventure 1

Adventure 2

Adventure 3

Ending

Solution

Epilog

3. Prune and Plump   **4. Polish and Re-Write**   **5. Publish and Perform**

Story Planner F

Story Title _____

1. Plot and Plan

Beginning

Characters
Setting
Problem
STAR Vocabulary

2. Package the First Draft (Write in tne boxes below.)

Middle

Adventure 1
Adventure 2
Adventure 3

Ending

Solution
Epilog

3. Prune and Plump (Erase or overwrite to revise the story.)

4. Polish and Re-Write (Write on your own paper.)

5. Publish and Perform

Story Planner G: White Elephant

Name _____

Date _____

1. Plot and Plan

Directions: A "white elephant" is something a person has but does not want. Develop a character and describe the "white elephant." In the middle, the character must try to get rid of the unwanted item but cannot. Plan the story ending and write how the character solves the problem. All stories have characters, setting, problem, and solution.

2. Package the First Draft (Write in the boxes below.)

Beginning: Introduce characters, setting, and the story problem.

Middle: Plan to write about three things that happen in the story before the character is able to solve the problem. Do not write the ending of the story in this section.

Ending: Plan the ending of the story. The characters solve the problem in the ending of a story.

3. Prune and Plump   4. Polish and Re-Write   5. Publish and Perform

Story Planner G: Frog Story

Name _____ Date _____

1. Plot and Plan

Directions: Plan a story about someone you misjudged at first but who turned out to be more of a prince than a frog. Develop and use STAR Vocabulary. Write in the first person, "I." Create the frog/prince character.

2. Package the First Draft (Write in the boxes below.)

Beginning: Introduce characters, setting, and the story problem.

Middle: Plan to write about three things that happen in the story before you changed your opinion of "Frog." Do not write the ending of the story in this section.

Ending: Plan the ending of the story. The characters solve the problem in the ending of a story.

3. Prune and Plump   4. Polish and Re-Write   5. Publish and Perform

Story Planner G: A Very Fishy Tale

Name _____

Date _____

1. Plot and Plan

Directions: Use exaggeration to plan a tall tale on Story Planner G below. Develop and use STAR Vocabulary. Draw a related picture on the back of this page.

2. Package the First Draft (Write in the boxes below.)

Beginning: Introduce characters, setting, and the story problem.

Middle: Plan three adventures for the characters as they try to solve the story problem. Do not solve the problem in the middle of the story.

Ending: Plan the ending of the story. The characters solve the problem in the ending of a story.

3. Prune and Plump   4. Polish and Re-Write   5. Publish and Perform

Story Planner G

Name _____

Date _____

Story Title _____

1. Plot and Plan: Choose a topic and develop a STAR Vocabulary list. Plan a story with a beginning, middle, and ending. All stories have characters, setting, problem, and solution.

2. Package the First Draft (Write in the boxes below.)

Beginning: Introduce characters, setting, and the story problem.

Middle: Plan to write about three things that happen in the story before the character is able to solve the problem. Do not write the ending of the story in this section.

Ending: Plan the ending of the story. The characters solve the problem in the ending of a story.

3. Prune and Plump (using page 189)   **4. Polish and Re-Write**   **5. Publish and Perform**

Generic Story Writing Frame 5

4. Polish and Re-write on the lines below

Story Title

Beginning

Middle

Ending

5. Publish and Perform

Story Planner H:
Cinderella Genre Framework

Name_____

Date_____

Genre: A story genre is a group of very similar stories. For example, there are hundreds of variations on the Cinderella story. Nearly every country has a culturally adapted version of the Cinderella classic story.

Directions: Read or listen to three different versions of the Cinderella story. Identify common attributes from all the stories and list them in the first column. Write notes about specific variations of those attributes in story columns 1, 2, and 3. In the last column, create a Cinderella story related to your own or local cultural heritage. The Cinderella character you create can be male or female.

1. Plot and Plan

Story Attribute	Story 1	Story 2	Story 3	Student Generated Story

Use as many copies of this matrix frame as needed or make your own.

Use Story Writing Frame 6 (pages 191–192) to write the story.

Generic Story Writing Frame 6

Name_____   Date_____

_____
Story Title

2. Package the First Draft

Beginning (The beginning introduces the *characters*, *setting*, and *problem*.)

_____

_____

_____

_____

_____

_____

_____

_____

Middle (The characters try to solve the problem during their adventures in the middle of the story.)

Adventure 1

_____

_____

_____

_____

_____

_____

_____

_____

_____

Generic Story Writing Frame 6 *(cont.)*

Adventure 2

_____

_____

_____

_____

_____

_____

_____

_____

Adventure 3

_____

_____

_____

_____

_____

_____

_____

_____

_____

Ending (Solve the problem in the ending of the story and write how things change as a result.)

_____

_____

_____

_____

_____

3. **Use Prune and Plump** from the Revise and Edit Check List.

4. **Use Polish and Re-Write** from the Revise and Edit Check List.

5. **Publish and Perform:** Share the story with others.

Story Planner H:
Genre Parallel Framework

Name_____   Date_____

_____
Title of Story

Genre: A story genre is a group of very similar stories with detail variations. Many fairy tales, western stories, Jack stories, Anansi stories, and folk tales belong to genres. Identify two or three stories that belong to a genre. Read or listen to the stories and write the story attributes in the boxes below. Decide on attributes to keep for a new story and write them in the last column. Use additional copies of this page if needed.

1. Plot and Plan

Story Attribute	Story 1	Story 2	Story 3	Student-Generated Story

Use as many copies of this matrix frame as needed or make your own.

Use Story Writing Frame 6 (pages 191–192) to write the story.

Trademark Character

Name_____   Date_____

Directions:

- Develop a Trademark Character who belongs to you alone. Do not copy a character already in existence. You may borrow traits from many sources to make a character who is uniquely yours. The new character becomes your Trademark Character.

- You will use the same character in many settings. He or she must always remain true to the traits you assign to him or her.

- Do not create an essentially bad or evil person. They are difficult to work with over long periods of time and in many of the assigned situations. You can add those characters as needed.

_____

Name of Character

Physical Attributes (Character's appearance)	**Personality Attributes** (Character's behaviors)	**Interests, Hobbies, and Interesting Experiences**
_____	_____	_____
_____	_____	_____
_____	_____	_____
_____	_____	_____
_____	_____	_____
_____	_____	_____

Draw the Trademark Character

Trademark Character's Family and Friends

(supporting characters)

Name_____   Date_____

_____ / _____
supporting character's name   relationship to main character

Physical Traits	Personality Traits	Interests and Hobbies

_____ / _____
supporting character's name   relationship to main character

Physical Traits	Personality Traits	Interests and Hobbies

_____ / _____
supporting character's name   relationship to main character

Physical Traits	Personality Traits	Interests and Hobbies

Other Information: _____

_____

Aliens for Lunch

(Trademark Story Kicker)

Name_____   Date_____

1. **Plot and Plan:** Create a story that involves aliens from outer space visiting the trademark character you created. Include a problem and solution with two to three events in the middle. Develop a STAR Vocabulary list for the story.

Draw the Alien	Draw and label the setting.	Write a short sentence about the problem of the story.

Draw and label three events in the middle of the story.		

Draw and label the solution to the problem.	Draw and label the epilog.

Aliens for Lunch (cont.)

(Trademark Story Kicker)

Name _____ Date _____

2. **Package the First Draft:** Follow the story plan from the previous page to write a first draft of the story, "Aliens for Lunch." Using quotation marks, write dialog that makes the story come to life. Remember to indent each time a speaker changes.

_____

_____

_____

_____

_____

_____

_____

_____

_____

_____

_____

_____

_____

_____

_____

_____

_____

_____

_____

_____

_____

Use another page if needed.

3. **Prune and Plump**   4. **Polish and Re-Write**   5. **Publish and Perform**

Trademark Story Kicker Blank

Name_____   Date_____

_____
Title of Story

1. **Plot and Plan:** Your teacher will assign a topic and story problem. The story will involve the Trademark Character you created. Develop a STAR Vocabulary list for the story. Follow the drawing plan below to plan the story.

Draw the _____	Draw and label the setting.	Write a short sentence about the problem of the story.

Draw and label three events in the middle of the story.		

Draw and label the solution to the problem.	Draw and label the epilog.

Trademark Story Kicker Writing Frame

Name_____   Date_____

_____
Story Title

2. Package the First Draft: Follow the story plan from the previous page to write a first draft of the story. Using quotation marks, write dialog that makes the story come to life. Remember to indent each time a speaker changes.

_____
_____
_____
_____
_____
_____
_____
_____
_____
_____
_____
_____
_____
_____
_____
_____
_____
_____
_____
_____
_____
_____
_____
_____

Use another page if needed.

3. Prune and Plump   4. Polish and Re-Write   5. Publish and Perform

Time Out

(Trademark Story Kicker)

Name_____   Date_____

Prompt: Read "Sleeping Beauty," "Rip Van Winkle," or "Buck Rogers." Write a story in which your trademark character was asleep, frozen, in another time zone, or in suspended animation for 100 years and then wakes up. Use Trademark Character Story Kicker Blank and Trademark Character Story Kicker Writing Frame for this writing assignment.

Guidelines:

- Explain how this phenomenon happened.
- The story must show how life changed in 100 years.
- The trademark character will find a friend who will help him or her in the new time.
- The trademark character will help solve a mystery.
- The trademark character will face dangers, adventures, and misadventures.
- The trademark character will adapt to life in the new time.

Title of Story

```

```

1. Plot and Plan

- Use the story prompt above to create the scenario, also called the plot, for the story.
- Develop a STAR vocabulary list (sensory, technical, articulate, realistic).
- Decide upon a location for the story.
- Conduct research on life 100 years ago. Make notes as necessary.
- Use vivid description and storytelling to describe the events in the story.
- Develop other characters for the story.
- Name the story.

2. Package the First Draft

- Write the first draft of the story on your own paper or use Trademark Characters Story Kickers Writing Frame.

3. Prune and Plump

- Use revision and editing strategies to improve the story.
- Have peers read, review, and make suggestions.
- Ask an adult to read, review, and make suggestions.

4. Polish and Re-Write

- Edit for grammar, mechanics, and spelling.
- Write a revised copy.

5. Publish and Perform

- Type on paper or use word processing.
- Submit to a publisher.
- Share with friends and family.
- Save in a scrapbook or portfolio.
- Post on a bulletin board or wall.

Tough

(Trademark Story Kicker)

Name_____   Date_____

Prompt: Write a story about a friend of the trademark character who has a tough time at home because the other members of the family are good athletes and are deeply involved in sports but he or she is not. Use Trademark Character Story Kicker Blank and Trademark Character Writing Frame for this assignment.

Guidelines:
- The friend feels inferior, intimidated, and lonely because he or she is not like the rest of the family.
- Use speaker's dialog with quotation marks to write the story.
- Speak in first person from the trademark character's point of view.
- The trademark character must help the friend find his or her true talents and develop.

Title of Story

1. **Plot and Plan**
   - Use the story prompt above to create the scenario, also called the plot, for the story.
   - Develop a STAR vocabulary list (sensory, technical, articulate, realistic).
   - Decide upon a location for the story.
   - Use vivid description and storytelling to describe the events in the story.
   - Develop other characters for the story.
   - Name the story.

2. **Package the First Draft**
   - Write the first draft of the story on your own paper or use Trademark Characters Story Kickers Writing Frame.

3. **Prune and Plump**
   - Use revision and editing strategies to improve the story.
   - Have peers read, review, and make suggestions.
   - Ask an adult to read, review, and make suggestions.

4. **Polish and Re-Write**
   - Edit for grammar, mechanics, and spelling.
   - Write a revised copy.

5. **Publish and Perform**
   - Type on paper or use word processing.
   - Submit to a publisher.
   - Save in a scrapbook or portfolio.
   - Post on a bulletin board or wall.
   - Share with friends and family.

Addicted

(Trademark Story Kicker)

Name_____   Date_____

Prompt: Write a Rapunzel genre story. Your trademark character is the forfeited child in the story. Use Trademark Character Story Kicker Blank and Trademark Character Writing Frame for this assignment.

Guidelines:

- One parent is addicted to something such as drugs, alcohol, or gambling, and this causes the family to make bad choices.
- The other parent or family members resort to stealing or other illegal activities to support the addiction.
- A child is taken from the family because of the addiction and behaviors of the family.
- The trademark character must make life decisions. He or she must decide either to follow in the footsteps of the family or make his or her own way in life.

Title of Story

[   ]

1. **Plot and Plan**

   - Use the story prompt above to create the scenario, also called the plot, for the story.
   - Develop a STAR vocabulary list (sensory, technical, articulate, realistic).
   - Decide upon a location for the story.
   - Use vivid description and storytelling to describe the events in the story.
   - Develop other characters for the story.
   - Name the story.

2. **Package the First Draft**

   - Write the first draft of the story on your own paper or use Trademark Characters Story Kicker Writing Frame.

3. **Prune and Plump**

   - Use revision and editing strategies to improve the story.
   - Have peers read, review, and make suggestions.
   - Ask an adult to read, review, and make suggestions.

4. **Polish and Re-Write**

   - Edit for grammar, mechanics, and spelling.
   - Write a revised copy.

5. **Publish and Perform**

   - Type on paper or use word processing.
   - Submit to a publisher.
   - Save in a scrapbook or portfolio.
   - Post on a bulletin board or wall.
   - Share with friends and family.

Affliction

(Trademark Story Kicker)

Name _____   Date _____

Prompt: Write a story about your trademark character's sick classmate.

Guidelines:
- The sick classmate has a serious, life threatening illness.
- The sick classmate's family is struggling with the illness and financial hardships.
- Doctors are trying new or alternative treatments for the illness.
- The trademark character must find ways to help the family.
- The trademark character motivates others to help the family.
- The sick classmate suffers depression because of the illness and sometimes vents the depression as anger on others.
- The trademark character becomes a real friend to the sick classmate.
- The fate of the sick classmate is up to you, the writer.

Title of Story

1. Plot and Plan
- Use the story prompt above to create the scenario, also called the plot, for the story.
- Develop a STAR vocabulary list (sensory, technical, articulate, realistic).
- Use Story Planner I to outline the story.
- Decide upon a location for the story.
- Use vivid description and storytelling to describe the events in the story.
- Develop other characters for the story.
- Name the story.

2. Package the First Draft
- Write the first draft of the story on your own paper or use Trademark Characters Story Kicker Writing Frame.

3. Prune and Plump
- Use revision and editing strategies to improve the story.
- Have peers read, review, and make suggestions.
- Ask an adult to read, review, and make suggestions.

4. Polish and Re-Write
- Edit for grammar, mechanics, and spelling.
- Write a revised copy.

5. Publish and Perform
- Type on paper or use word processing.
- Submit to a publisher.
- Save in a scrapbook or portfolio.
- Post on a bulletin board or wall.
- Share with friends and family.

Story Planner I

Name _____

Date _____

Beginning	Middle	Ending
Problem: (What problems do the characters need to solve in the story?) _____ _____ _____ _____ _____	Adventure A _____ _____ _____ _____ _____	**Solution:** (How is the problem solved?) _____ _____ _____ _____ _____ _____
Characters: (Make webs that describe the characters. Write their names in the center.)	Adventure B _____ _____ _____ _____ _____	**Epilog:** (What happens to the characters later, after the problem was solved?) _____ _____ _____ _____ _____
Setting: (Describe the setting: when and where the story takes place.) _____ _____ _____ _____	Adventure C _____ _____ _____ _____ _____	

Point of View

(Trademark Story Kicker)

Name_____   Date_____

Prompt: Re-write a fairy tale from the point of view of the villain. Place your trademark character in the story. Use Story Planner I.

Guidelines:
- The villain explains away all his crimes from his point of view.
- The villain believes it is his or her right to commit the crimes.
- Write the story in dialect or vernacular familiar to you. (Examples: slang, technology speech, cook's speech, policeman's speech, CB speech)
- Use humor.

Title of Story

1. **Plot and Plan**
   - Use the story prompt above to create the scenario, also called the plot, for the story.
   - Develop a STAR vocabulary list (sensory, technical, articulate, realistic).
   - Decide upon a location for the story.
   - Use vivid description and storytelling to describe the events in the story.
   - Develop other characters for the story.
   - Name the story.

2. **Package the First Draft**
   - Write the first draft of the story on your own paper or use Trademark Characters Story Kicker Writing Frame.

3. **Prune and Plump**
   - Use revision and editing strategies to improve the story.
   - Have peers read, review, and make suggestions.
   - Ask an adult to read, review, and make suggestions.

4. **Polish and Re-Write**
   - Edit for grammar, mechanics, and spelling.
   - Write a revised copy.

5. **Publish and Perform**
   - Type on paper or use word processing.
   - Submit to a publisher.
   - Save in a scrapbook or portfolio.
   - Post on a bulletin board or wall.
   - Share with friends and family.

Bully

(Trademark Story Kicker)

Name _____   Date _____

Prompt: Write a story about bullying. Your trademark character is either the victim or a witness to the bullying. Use Story Planner I.

Guidelines:

- The bullying must take place in more than one setting.
- The bully will have a partner or a group of accomplices.
- The bully is manipulative with authority figures.
- The bully is sneaky and gets away with his behavior for a while.
- The bully makes unreasonable demands of the victims.
- The victim and witnesses will eventually stand up for themselves.

Title of Story

\[\]

1. **Plot and Plan**
   - Use the story prompt above to create the scenario, also called the plot, for the story.
   - Develop a STAR vocabulary list (sensory, technical, articulate, realistic).
   - Decide upon a location for the story.
   - Use vivid description and storytelling to describe the events in the story.
   - Develop other characters for the story.
   - Name the story.

2. **Package the First Draft**
   - Write the first draft of the story on your own paper or use Trademark Characters Story Kicker Writing Frame.

3. **Prune and Plump**
   - Use revision and editing strategies to improve the story.
   - Have peers read, review, and make suggestions.
   - Ask an adult to read, review, and make suggestions.

4. **Polish and Re-Write**
   - Edit for grammar, mechanics, and spelling.
   - Write a revised copy.

5. **Publish and Perform**
   - Type on paper or use word processing.
   - Submit to a publisher.
   - Save in a scrapbook or portfolio.
   - Post on a bulletin board or wall.
   - Share with friends and family.

Cinderella Again

(Trademark Story Kicker)

Name_____   Date_____

Prompt: Write a Cinderella genre story starring your trademark character. Use Story Planner I to plan the story.

Guidelines:

- Your trademark character has a step-parent and step-siblings who treat him or her badly.
- The trademark character has a dream or goal that he or she wants to fulfill.
- The step-siblings want the same thing for themselves.
- The trademark character has fine character qualities that shine even in adversity.
- The trademark character has an unusual advocate who helps in times of trouble.
- The trademark character triumphs in the end and achieves the goals.

Title of Story

1. **Plot and Plan**
   - Use the story prompt above to create the scenario, also called the plot, for the story.
   - Develop a STAR vocabulary list (sensory, technical, articulate, realistic).
   - Decide upon a location for the story.
   - Use vivid description and storytelling to describe the events in the story.
   - Develop other characters for the story.
   - Name the story.

2. **Package the First Draft**
   - Write the first draft of the story on your own paper or use Trademark Characters Story Kicker Writing Frame.

3. **Prune and Plump**
   - Use revision and editing strategies to improve the story.
   - Have peers read, review, and make suggestions.
   - Ask an adult to read, review, and make suggestions.

4. **Polish and Re-Write**
   - Edit for grammar, mechanics, and spelling.
   - Write a revised copy.

5. **Publish and Perform**
   - Type on paper or use word processing.
   - Submit to a publisher.
   - Save in a scrapbook or portfolio.
   - Post on a bulletin board or wall.
   - Share with friends and family.

Dishonest

(Trademark Story Kicker)

Name_____   Date_____

Prompt: Write a story about a time your trademark character became aware that a classmate was cheating, stealing, or otherwise being dishonest. Use Story Planner I.

Guidelines:
- Examine your character's feelings about cheating.
- Your character must also turn down the temptation to cheat.
- The trademark character must go against popular or powerful students in order to prevent the classmate from cheating or copying from him/her.
- The character avoids publicly embarrassing or turning in the cheating classmate.
- In a positive and helpful way, the trademark character must deal with the classmate's need to cheat.
- Write in first person, past tense point of view.

Title of Story

_____

1. Plot and Plan
- Use the story prompt above to create the scenario, also called the plot, for the story.
- Develop a Star vocabulary list (sensory, technical, articulate, realistic).
- Decide upon a location for the story.
- Use vivid description and storytelling to describe the events in the story.
- Develop other characters for the story.
- Name the story.

2. Package the First Draft
- Write the first draft of the story on your own paper or use Trademark Characters Story Kicker Writing Frame.

3. Prune and Plump
- Use revision and editing strategies to improve the story.
- Have peers read, review, and make suggestions.
- Ask an adult to read, review, and make suggestions.

4. Polish and Re-Write
- Edit for grammar, mechanics, and spelling.
- Write a revised copy.

5. Publish and Perform
- Type on paper or use word processing.
- Submit to a publisher.
- Save in a scrapbook or portfolio.
- Post on a bulletin board or wall.
- Share with friends and family.

Foreclosed

(Trademark Story Kicker)

Name _____   Date _____

Prompt: Write a story about factories, businesses, and jobs closing down in the region. The trademark character's family is forced to move because one or both of the parents have lost jobs. Write a realistic story about the things that happen in their lives. Use Story Planner I.

Guidelines:

- The job market suddenly closes down without warning.
- The family uses up all their resources.
- The family members lose their home when they cannot pay mortgage payments.
- The bank sends a policeman to order them to leave.
- The family has no relatives that can or will help them.
- One parent has some sickness.
- All family members suffer emotional distress over the ordeal.

Title of Story

_____

1. **Plot and Plan**
   - Use the story prompt above to create the scenario, also called the plot, for the story.
   - Develop a STAR vocabulary list (sensory, technical, articulate, realistic).
   - Decide upon a location for the story.
   - Use vivid description and storytelling to describe the events in the story.
   - Develop other characters for the story.
   - Name the story.

2. **Package the First Draft**
   - Write the first draft of the story on your own paper or use Trademark Characters Story Kicker Writing Frame.

3. **Prune and Plump**
   - Use revision and editing strategies to improve the story.
   - Have peers read, review, and make suggestions.
   - Ask an adult to read, review, and make suggestions.

4. **Polish and Re-Write**
   - Edit for grammar, mechanics, and spelling.
   - Write a revised copy.

5. **Publish and Perform**
   - Type on paper or use word processing.
   - Submit to a publisher.
   - Save in a scrapbook or portfolio.
   - Post on a bulletin board or wall.
   - Share with friends and family.

The Choice

(Trademark Story Kicker)

Name_____   Date_____

Prompt: Read "The Little Mermaid." Write a Little Mermaid genre story starring your trademark character. Use Story Planner I.

Guidelines:

- The character must leave the familiar and go to another realm or environment.
- The character will meet a being from that place and decide to give up all that is familiar in order to live in the realm or environment of that being.
- The character will face dangers.
- The character will face anger from others.

Title of Story

1. **Plot and Plan**
   - Use the story prompt above to create the scenario, also called the plot, for the story.
   - Develop a STAR vocabulary list (sensory, technical, articulate, realistic).
   - Decide upon a location for the story.
   - Use vivid description and storytelling to describe the events in the story.
   - Develop other characters for the story.
   - Name the story.

2. **Package the First Draft**
   - Write the first draft of the story on your own paper or use Trademark Characters Story Kickers Writing Frame.

3. **Prune and Plump**
   - Use revision and editing strategies to improve the story.
   - Have peers read, review, and make suggestions.
   - Ask an adult to read, review, and make suggestions.

4. **Polish and Re-Write**
   - Edit for grammar, mechanics, and spelling.
   - Write a revised copy.

5. **Publish and Perform**
   - Type on paper or use word processing.
   - Submit to a publisher.
   - Save in a scrapbook or portfolio.
   - Post on a bulletin board or wall.
   - Share with friends and family.

Introduction to Poetry, Letters, and Self-Reflection

Poetry Patterns

Students can copy poetry patterns to create poetry of their own. Copy and distribute copies of Poetry Patterns (pages 214–216). Especially helpful as examples for modeling are the quatrain, cinquain, limerick, and haiku. All of these require practice to develop a facility with meter, rhythm, and brevity. Sustained practice and guidance, however, will pay off in increased self-confidence for the young writers. After students create poetry, help them edit for corrections and then post the poetry samples on bulletin boards or publish in a school newspaper.

Prose to Poetry: "Sandstorm"

Essays are good sources for poetry. Copy and distribute copies of "Sandstorm," prose form and poetry form (pages 217–218). Read the prose version normally—like natural speech. Then, read the poetry version, pausing at all the line breaks. Compare the two written works. Notice that most line breaks occurred at the beginning of prepositional phrases. Copy and distribute Prepositions and More About Prepositions from Chapter 2, Vocabulary (pages 30–31).

Direct students to select a reflective essay from their portfolios or ring binders and change it into poetry by breaking it down into phrases. Use centering and columns to give the new work a poetry "look."

Alliteration: "Grouchy Sarah B."

Read the poem "Grouchy Sarah B" (page 220) three times. Alliteration is an author's craft that uses a repeated sound in a written selection. The author uses alliteration to help establish the rhythm of the poem and for the enjoyment of the way it sounds. Select a topic and write a poem using the same line patterns, line breaks, and applying alliteration. Poems with heavy alliteration are frequently humorous.

Suggestions: Happy Harold T; Nosy Nellie Nee; Helpful Harriet Lee; Bumbling Barry Burn; Clumsy Clive McClee; Forgetful Francis McFly; Smelly Smithers Small; and Grave Gracie Green.

Teach Poetry: "Nellie in Her 'No!' Suit"

Display or project on the overhead a copy of the poem. Distribute copies of the poem, "Nellie in Her 'No' Suit" (page 219).

Teach: Oral Importance of Poetry

- Read the poem to the class.

- Involve students in choral reading of the poem.

- Ask individual students to read the poem aloud.

- Ask students to identify rhyming words.

Introduction to Poetry, Letters, and Self-Reflection *(cont.)*

Teach: Explain and Discuss "Play on Words"

- "Snow" and "no" are similar. "No" is found inside the word *snow*. A young child might substitute the word *no* for the word *snow*.

- Ask students to speculate why the author used the words, "playing in the no."

- Students might reply:

  —It's a child's way of saying *snow*.

  —It's a child resisting something she did not want to do.

  —It's the author's play on words, saying that Nellie was experimenting with saying "no" to her parents.

Teach: Important Distinctions

- "it's" is the contraction of *it is* or *it has*

- "its" is a possessive pronoun

Teach: Semicolon and Compound Sentences

- Three compound sentences use semicolons to take the place of conjunctions.

- Ask students which conjunction could fit in each compound sentence instead of the semicolon.

- Model practice compound sentences using semicolons.

- Ask students to supply compound sentences using a semicolon.

Teach: Quotation Marks

- Review quotation marks around spoken dialog.

- Point to quotation dialog examples in the poem.

Teach: Concluding Observations

- Ask students if they have ever been over-dressed and sent out to play.

- Assign students to write descriptive sentences about that experience. Share those sentences with the class.

- *Nellie* and *no* are examples of alliteration because of the initial "n" sound. Ask students for reasons the author chose Nellie for the name of the character.

Creating Class Poems

- Brainstorm: Lead the class to brainstorm a list of ideas about the theme of a person or animal having to do something he or she does not like to do. *Examples:* eating prunes, giving (or getting) a dog bath, going to the doctor for a shot, cleaning one's room, etc.

- Follow the pattern or a pattern similar to "Nellie in Her 'No!' Suit."

- Follow the writing process sequence on the following page.

Introduction to Poetry, Letters, and Self-Reflection *(cont.)*

First Draft

Students or pairs of students will choose a topic from the brainstormed list and use short sentences to give a description of the hated activity.

Require each poem to include the following elements:

- "it's" as a contraction
- "its" as a possessive pronoun
- a compound sentence with semicolon

Revising Conference

- Hold conferences with students and make suggestions for improvements in the poems. Look for opportunities to help students "play" with words like *no* and *snow* in the Nellie poem. (Lists of rhyming words sometimes help.)
- Direct students to write a second draft with improvements. Students should review work for errors. Students may use peer review.

Editing Conference

- Review student work for errors and make final suggestions.
- This is the time to refine for spelling, punctuation, and capitalization.

Final Draft: **Students write a final draft for publication.**

Publish

- Display, read aloud, store to disk, store in a journal, or read the poem to a relative.
- Optional: Word Processing—teach centering for poetry lines. Do not allow students to print a work until it has been edited and approved.
- Instruct students to illustrate the poems or to experiment with clip art.

Last Instruction

Poetry is supposed to be fun, so be an example to students and have fun with poetry!

Letters, Notes, and Invitations

Use the prompt-response blank to write an invitation. Use writing process steps to improve and edit the invitation and then write a final copy on the form provided, card stock, or a commercially prepared invitation. Word processing programs can be used to print the final version.

Dear Gabby and Sage Advice from Sadie.

Assign students to become advice columnists and write answers to questions. As a class project, follow up by asking students to write letters seeking advice to an advice columnist.

Self-Reflection

Self is a popular topic among students. Read directions on each page and guide students through the writing process according to their achievement level in writing.

Poetry Patterns

Alphabet

by Jima Dunigan

Carefree

Dolphins

Even

Flip

Gracefully

by _____

_____

_____

_____

_____

_____

Acrostic

by Jima Dunigan

Fierce

Righteous

Energetic

Dude

by _____

C _____

O _____

O _____

L _____

Concrete *(special shape or design)*
by Jima Dunigan

by _____

LEAVES
Dizzy
FALL
to the ground.

My cup of Tea

Quatrain *(four-line stanza with rhyming lines)*

Ghost Town 1

by Jima Dunigan

Not far west of Wyoming there lies

A little town that men despise.

The streets that once glittered with gold

Now are barren, dusty and cold.

by _____

_____

_____

_____

_____

Definition *(not necessary to rhyme, any length)*

Friendship

by Jima Dunigan

snow

fleas

homework

family

work

success

Homework

by Jima Dunigan

hard

tedious

boring

learning

mastering

confidence

Caterpillar

by Jima Dunigan

crawly

creepy

leggy

long

fuzzy

frightening

by _____

_____

_____

_____

_____

_____

Poetry Patterns *(cont.)*

Cinquain *(five lines)*

One-word title	**Blankets**	**Soup**
	by Jima Dunigan	by _____
Two describing words	Snuggly, soft	_____
Three action words	Heating, comforting, cuddling	_____
Four feeling words	Warming body and soul	_____
One synonym for the title	Comforter	_____

Limerick *(five lines)*

	Boy from Rome	**Girl from Spain**
	by Jima Dunigan	by _____
Lines 1, 2, 5 rhyme	There once was a boy from Rome	_____
Lines 3, 4 rhyme	Who could not find a home.	_____
	He searched and he tried	_____
	'till he found a bride.	_____
	They made a home of their own.	_____

Haiku *(three sensible lines—about nature)*

	Footprints	**Water**
	by Jima Dunigan	by Jima Dunigan
Line 1—five syllables	See the red berries	Watch the water flow
Line 2—seven syllables	fallen like little footprints	down through valley and ravine
Line 3—five syllables	on the garden snow.	seeking ocean home.

5 Ws

	My Dog	**Please Write**	**My Friend**
	by Jima Dunigan	by Jima Dunigan	by _____
Who:	My dog	Teacher	My friend
What:	curls up	says write	_____
When:	every night	each day	_____
Where:	on my bed	in school	_____
Why:	because I let him.	to master the art.	_____

Poetry Patterns *(cont.)*

Pools

by Jima Dunigan

Pools are for kids.
Pools are for grownups, too.
Pools are for swimming.
Pools are for cooling down.
Pools are for floating.
Pools are serene.
Pools are for splashing.
Pools are wild and inviting.
Pools are for diving, if its safe.

Pools at home are for parties
　　and gatherings
　　and late night soaks to relieve
　　the stress of the day.

Pools in a field are lovely,
　　delicious, and delightful.
Pools make good pictures to paint.

Pools are good for skating in winter.
　　when ice freezes over.
Pools are good for the fish, turtles,
　　snakes, frogs, and insects.

Hills

by _____

_____
_____
_____
_____
_____
_____
_____
_____
_____
_____
_____
_____
_____
_____
_____
_____
_____
_____

The Carnival

by Jima Dunigan

The Carnival is:

　　　Loud,

　　　　　Laughing,

　　　　　　　Loitering,

　　Bright,

　　　　　Bustling,

　　　　　　　Boisterous,

　　Food,

　　　　　Friends,

　　　　　　　Fantasy,

　　Exciting,

　　　　　Entertaining,

　　　　　　　Expensive

　　Fun!

Picnics

by _____

Picnics are

　　_____

　　　　_____

　　　　　　_____

　　_____

　　　　_____

　　　　　　_____

　　_____

　　　　_____

　　　　　　_____

　　_____

　　　　_____

　　　　　　_____

　　_____

Sandstorm

by Jima Dunigan

I was standing in line at the fence, waiting for the big yellow bus to come back from its first run and take me home. I always stood in line, though others played their last minutes. But I, having once missed the bus, stood and waited with the other nervous line keepers.

I was wearing my white coat, the one I got in second grade. My mother had bought it large enough to last. I was a neat and careful child, so the coat was not overly worn. It still looked nice to my eyes. I did not mind. I liked it. The air was chilly enough for a coat; for fall was just beginning and I was in fifth grade.

No one expected it: not those who were playing, not the nervous line keepers, not the teachers, not the yellow dog who always came at home time to romp with willing children. It came anyway, beating my body and everyone else's—slapping, stinging, whirling, and roaring.

A small whirlwind had come upon us. With it came a ton of sand.

I closed my eyes. I turned my back to the force of it. I crouched low. I do not know what the others did. I did not dare open my eyes—not until later.

The twister roared its way through the schoolyard; not strong enough to pick us up, but plenty strong. It ripped papers from my hand; papers I was taking home to show. It slapped me with twigs, branches, and other unknown objects. As the wind abated, I sneaked a peek and saw a multitude of objects cart-wheeling through the air and on the ground. Then, thankfully, the storm was finished. I could see it charging toward the end of the valley, armed and ready to blast into someone else's life.

I opened my eyes wider and looked through sandy lashes. I carefully took sandy fingers to tap the sand from my eyes, and my brow, and my hair. Then I shook my coat. Another sandstorm burst from it and fell to the ground. I emptied my coat pockets, my shoes, and even my socks. I could feel sand inside my clothing, my nose, and my ears. I could see other children ridding themselves of sand. Some of the boys were shouting from the exhilaration the storm had visited on them. I admit, I felt some of it myself.

I scanned the playground for Yellow Dog. I never did see him again after that day. Perhaps the wind swept him away and rained him down on some other community. Dorothy and Toto came to my mind. I was too young to realize how serious things could have been.

The playground was littered with whatever had been stolen somewhere back in the path of the whirlwind. I saw a bus duty teacher looking over the mess, shaking his head.

I have not seen another whirlwind in all my days. I hope I never do. Once was enough.

Sandstorm

by Jima Dunigan

I was standing in line at the fence,
waiting for the big yellow bus
to come back from its first run
and take me home.
I always stood in line,
though others played their last minutes.
But I, having once missed the bus,
stood and waited
with the other nervous line keepers.
I was wearing my white coat,
the one I got in second grade.
My mother
had bought it large enough to last.
I was a neat and careful child,
so the coat was not overly worn.
It still looked nice to my eyes.
I did not mind.
I liked it.
The air was chilly enough for a coat,
for fall was just beginning
and I was in fifth grade.
No one expected it:
not those who were playing,
not the nervous line keepers,
not the teachers,
not the yellow dog
who always came
at home time
to romp with willing children.
It came anyway,
beating my body and everyone else's—
slapping, stinging, whirling, and
roaring.
A small whirlwind had come upon us.
With it came a ton of sand.
I closed my eyes.
I turned my back to the force of it.
I crouched low.
I do not know what the others did.
I did not dare open my eyes—
not until later.
The twister roared its way
through the school-yard;
not strong enough to pick us up,
but plenty strong.
It ripped papers from my hand;
papers I was taking home to show.
It slapped me with twigs, branches,

and other unknown objects.
As the wind abated,
I sneaked a peek
and saw a multitude of objects
cart-wheeling through the air
and on the ground.
Then, thankfully, the storm was
finished.
I could see it charging
toward the end of the valley,
armed and ready
to blast into someone else's life.
I opened my eyes wider
and looked through sandy lashes.
I carefully took sandy fingers
to tap the sand from my eyes,
and my brow, and my hair.
Then I shook my coat.
Another sandstorm burst from it
and fell to the ground.
I emptied my coat pockets,
my shoes, and even my socks.
I could feel sand inside my clothing,
my nose, and my ears.
I could see other children
ridding themselves of sand.
Some of the boys were shouting
from the exhilaration the storm
had visited on them.
I admit, I felt some of it myself.
I scanned the playground
for Yellow Dog.
I never did see him again after that day.
Perhaps the wind swept him away
and rained him down
on some other community.
Dorothy and Toto came to my mind.
I was too young to realize
how serious things could have been.
The playground was littered
with whatever had been stolen
somewhere back in the path
of the whirlwind.
I saw a bus duty teacher
looking over the mess, shaking his head.
I have not seen another whirlwind
in all my days. I hope I never do.
Once was enough.

Nellie in Her "No!" Suit

by

Jima Dunigan

Nellie went playing

in the "no."

"No, I won't slide.

No, I won't skate.

No, to snow angels.

It's snow I hate!"

"It's cold.

It's frozen.

Its crunch grits

my teeth.

I can't bend over;

I can't see my feet."

"I'm much too bundled;

I can't lift my arms.

This scarf is stifling;

I'm much too warm!"

"I'm stuck here behind;

the big kids won't wait.

Nellie in her no-suit said,

"It's snow I hate!"

Grouchy Sarah B

by
Jima Dunigan

Sarah B.
was grouchy all day,
and yesterday,
and the other day,
and the before that day

But, not today!
She had growled,
and scowled,
and howled,
and ow-ed

—but, not today—

and grumped,
and bumped,
and hit,
and, oh my, bit,
and grouched,
and ouched

—but, not today—

Today, Sarah B.
promised to be,
good as can be,
to smile
a while
and show some teeth
and sing a song
how good it will be!
Believe me!
It's been too long.

How lovely,
Miss Sarah B.

_____

_____

_____

_____

_____

_____

_____

_____

_____

_____

_____

_____

_____

_____

_____

_____

_____

_____

_____

_____

_____

_____

_____

_____

_____

_____

Invitation

Name _____   Date _____

Step 1: Plot and Plan

- Use the Prompt-Response frame to write an invitation.
- Use one or two transitional words to lead the reader from one idea to another.
- Use the gray boxes for proper positioning of date, salutation, closing, punctuation, and signatures.

Step 2: Package the First Draft

Prompt	Response
Write the date in the gray box to the right.	
Write the salutation in the gray box. Put a comma in the small box after the salutation.	
Write a sentence that tells the reader that you are inviting him or her to the event, Name the event.	
Write a sentence that tells the reader the purpose of the event.	
Write a sentence that tells the reader the time, date, and place of the event.	
Write a sentence that tells the reader if the event is formal or informal so they will know what to wear.	
Include other information, as necessary, in this sentence.	
Write a closing in the gray box. Put a comma after the closing.	
Write your name in the gray box. If you are very well acquainted, use only your first name.	

Invitation *(cont.)*

Step 3. Prune and Plump   **4. Polish and Re-Write**

Erase or use a different colored marker or pen to make corrections and revisions. Over-write on the prompt response frame. Your teacher may direct you to use peer editing.

Prune and Plump	Polish
Use this checklist for revising the first draft	Use this checklist for editing before final draft
___ beginning, middle, ending	___ clear word choice
___ clearly defined topic	___ transition
___ adequate support	___ subject/verb agreement
___ complete unfinished supporting details	___ STAR Vocabulary
___ ideas in order	___ to the point
___ easy to follow, logical	___ adjectives
___ varied sentence beginnings	___ adverbs
___ Improve each sentence.	___ redundancy
___ Does the writing say what you intended to say?	___ punctuation
___ Look for obvious mistakes and correct them.	___ spelling
___ Think about what others say.	___ capitals
___ transitional words	
___ vivid description	Re-write a clean copy of the invitation on the card below.
___ who, what, when, where, why, how	

5. Publish: Cut out the card below. Decorate the left side and the front. Send the card. Option: Write the invitation on a commercially printed and decorated card.

Dear Gabby

(Advice Column)

Name_____   Date_____

Dear Gabby,

I have a problem, and I would like your advice.
I am thirteen years old. Jamie, one of the most
popular people in school is in one of my
classes. We like each other. We can not really
date, but we have lots of opportunities to talk
because we are in the same school and youth
group. It is exciting to me since this is my first
romance. I talked about it a lot to my best
friend. I invited my friend along for several
events. The first thing I know, my friend is also
interested in my love interest. My friend is
doing everything possible to take my place.
Now that I am thinking about it, I realize every
time I do something new, get something new, or
win an award, that my friend makes it a mission
to upstage me. I never minded much until now.
I still like my friend, but I feel upset. I still like
my boyfriend. My mom says imitation is
flattery. She also says my friend is a little
jealous of me. What is a person to do in this
situation? I do not want a cute, short answer.
Give me some real help.

Puzzled in Seventh

Dear Puzzled,

_____

_____

_____

_____

_____

_____

_____

_____

Dear Gabby,

I am eleven, in the sixth grade. Since no one
really knows who is writing this, I can ask some
straight questions and I want some straight
answers. I will admit up front I have not
exactly been an angel. I tried smoking and got
caught. I sneaked out of the house a couple of
times and, you guessed it, I got caught. I have
been caught every single time I tried something
I wasn't allowed to do. I'm not a bad kid, I just
want to know about life. Now to the problem.
Now, Mom reads my diary and sometimes
listens in on my phone. She has screened the
Internet, and she snoops in my room. I feel like
I am being treated like a baby, and it makes me
very angry. Do you have advice?

Caught Red-handed

Dear Caught,

_____

_____

_____

_____

_____

_____

_____

_____

_____

_____

_____

_____

Sage Advice from Sadie

(Advice Column)

Name_____   Date_____

Assignment: Design a graphic organizer and plan how Sadie will answer the letter from Alex. Write the answer in letter form. Notice that Alex has two problems to be answered.

Dear Sadie,

My mom won't give me any privacy at all. She snoops in my room. I know she does because she knows everything about me, even things I do not tell her. I can tell she reads my diary because I made up a phony diary with phony friends and wrote that I shoplifted with them just to see if she was reading it. Sure enough, she gave me a long lecture about choosing friends wisely and about what would happen if I shoplifted. She just can't be trusted. What should I do?

Another thing—she is always nagging me about cleaning up my room and getting my clothes down to the laundry room. She even expects me to fold laundry and take out the trash. I don't have much time for housework because I have homework and I have to practice sports so I can get a scholarship. She is a stay-at-home mom. I think taking care of the house is her job.

I really need privacy, and I need for my mom to stay off my back about the house. What can I say to get her to understand how I feel?

Alex

Dear Alex,

_____
_____
_____
_____
_____
_____
_____
_____
_____
_____
_____
_____
_____
_____
_____
_____
_____
_____
_____
_____
_____
_____
_____

ABCs of My Identity

Name_____   Date_____

Directions: On each line below, write a statement about an attribute of yours that begins with that letter. On line A for example, one might write "My greatest **ambition** in life has been . . .

A _____

_____

B _____

C _____

D _____

E _____

F _____

G _____

H _____

I _____

J _____

K _____

L _____

M _____

N _____

O _____

P _____

Q _____

R _____

S _____

T _____

U _____

V _____

W _____

X _____

Y _____

Z _____

Me, Myself, and I

Name_____

Date_____

Choose four important people in your life. Write the name of each person inside a bubble and write information about each one on the lines. Draw additional lines as needed. On another page, write paragraphs about each person, starting with yourself.

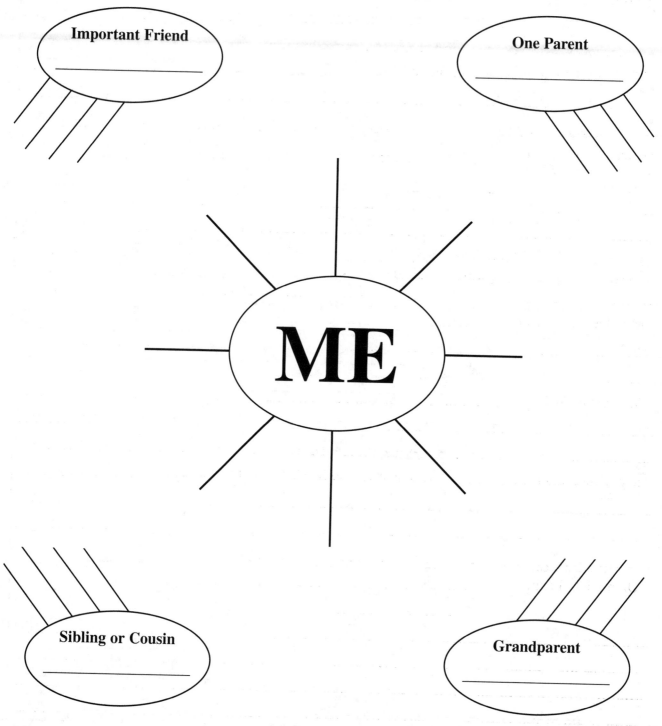

Important Friend
_____

One Parent
_____

ME

Sibling or Cousin
_____

Grandparent
_____

Me, Myself, and I (cont.)

(Reflections and Projections)

Name_____   Date_____

Based upon my personal choices, this is what my life could be like:

During high school, I will study _____

_____

_____

Also, during high school, I hope to achieve _____

_____

_____

After high school, I will study _____

_____

_____

_____

My spouse and I will probably have _____ (child, children). I imagine _____

boy(s) and _____ girl(s). I like the names _____ , _____ ,

_____ , _____ , _____, and _____ .

My oldest child will _____

_____

_____

My next child will _____

_____

_____

My spouse and I will probably buy a house. This is what I want in a house: _____

_____

_____

_____

On my job, I expect _____

_____

_____

_____

_____

Me, Myself, and I (cont.)

(Reflections and Projections)

I will be this kind of parent: _____

_____

_____

_____

_____

_____

I will not be this kind of parent: _____

_____

_____

_____

_____

_____

_____

I rate these things most valuable in life:_____

_____

_____

_____

_____

_____

The person who has influenced me most in life is_____

_____

_____

_____

_____

_____

Me, Myself, and I (cont.)

(Priorities Prioritized)

Name_____   Date_____

Many things are important to you in your life. In the box below, quickly write 20 to 30 words that represent the things that matter most to you. Then, on the lines below, list those things in the order of importance starting with one (1) being most important and ending with twenty (20) being least important. You may elect not to use some of the items you have written in the box. As you prioritize your list, you may strike through words from the box as you use them.

1. _____   11. _____
2. _____   12. _____
3. _____   13. _____
4. _____   14. _____
5. _____   15. _____
6. _____   16. _____
7. _____   17. _____
8. _____   18. _____
9. _____   19. _____
10. _____   20. _____

Write a short paragraph telling why you value most the items listed in the first five numbers.

_____

_____

_____

Me, Myself, and I (cont.)

(Income and Mortgage)

Name_____   Date_____

Salary

I am _____ old. I have chosen _____ as a career. My salary

will be $ _____. I will pay _____ approximately 25% in taxes and other

deductions to the government and keep 75% as take-home pay. My take-home pay will be

approximately $ _____ per year. Divided by 12 months, my monthly take-home pay will

be approximately $ _____. If I am married and my spouse works, we should double our

income. Together our take-home pay for a year will be $ _____ or $ _____

each month.

My House

We will buy a (house, mobile home, condominium) _____ for our family. The

bank allows two years' household income as a guideline for deciding how much a family can spend on

a house. Using that guideline, we can afford a house that costs $ _____. A typical

mortgage term for a large house is thirty years. A house payment is required each month. Twelve

months times thirty years equals _____ months. A typical mortgage

amount is usually calculated by multiplying the cost of the house times 3. The house I chose was

advertised for a cost of $ _____. Multiplied times three, my house will cost a total of $

_____. To find out how much I have to pay for each monthly payment, I divide the

mortgage amount by 360 monthly payments. My house payment will cost $ _____ each

month.

Autobiography, Biography Planner

Name_____   Date_____

Auto = self   **Bio** = life   **Graph** = write or draw

Choose the person for whom you wish to write a biography. He or she can be a famous person with materials and research available, or someone you know. It may be you. If you choose to write about yourself, it is an autobiography. Use the chronologically sequenced boxes below to create an autobiography.

1. Birth

Name_____
Boy _____ Girl _____
Date of birth _____
Length at birth_____
Weight at birth _____
Place of birth_____
Mother_____
Father _____
Sister _____
Brother _____

2. Firsts

First Word _____
First Birthday _____
_____
_____
_____
_____

3. Relatives

_____
_____
_____
_____
_____

4. Pre-school Experiences

_____
_____
_____
_____
_____
_____

5. Kindergarten

_____
_____
_____
_____
_____
_____

6. First Grade Experiences

_____
_____
_____
_____
_____

(For more, continue on the back of this page.)

New Year's Resolutions

Name_____ Date_____

Some people choose New Year's Day to make promises to themselves about changes they want to make in their lives. Below, write ten **resolutions** and tell why you want to make these changes in your life.

My Resolutions and Why

1. _____

_____

_____

2. _____

_____

_____

3. _____

_____

_____

4. _____

_____

_____

5. _____

_____

_____

6. _____

_____

_____

7. _____

_____

_____

8. _____

_____

_____

9. _____

_____

_____

10. _____

_____

_____

Developing Relationships 1

Name_____   Date_____

On the spaces below, name your friends and describe them and the relationship you have with each.

My Friends	Description of the Friend and the Relationship
_____	_____
	_____
	_____
_____	_____
	_____
	_____
_____	_____
	_____
	_____
_____	_____
	_____
	_____
_____	_____
	_____
	_____
_____	_____
	_____

Developing Relationships 2

Name _____

Date _____

On the spaces below, name persons with whom you would like to have a better relationship. Please tell why and how the relationship could improve.

Person	Why and How the Relationship Could Improve
_____	_____
	_____
	_____
	_____
_____	_____
	_____
	_____
	_____
_____	_____
	_____
	_____
	_____
_____	_____
	_____
	_____
	_____
_____	_____
	_____
	_____
	_____
_____	_____

A Healthy Body

Name_____   Date_____

Step 1. Plot and Plan: Use the graphic organizer below to prepare to write an essay that tells about three important things you can do now to ensure that you will have a healthy body. Be sure to give plenty of evidence to support the three choices. Use the STAR Vocabulary sheet from chapter two, page 22.

- Use the three sub-topics provided for you: *Exercise Often, Eat a Balanced Diet,* and *Smile Often.*
- The three sub-topics have been listed in the large boxes at the top of the columns.
- Under the sub-topics, create a list of related supporting details.

Guided Writing Note: Your teacher may guide you through the writing process. Do not go ahead of the class without instructions to do so.

Body Paragraph 1	Body Paragraph 2	Body Paragraph 3
(Exercise Often)	*(Eat a Balanced Diet)*	*(Smile Often)*

A Healthy Body *(cont.)*

Step 2. Package the First Draft

Writing the Introductory Paragraph

1. Build *background*: Write an attention-getting sentence or write about an incident related to the main idea.

2. Write a sentence that tells the *main idea* and the three sub-topic ideas.

3. Remember to indent.

_____

_____

_____

_____

_____

_____

Write Body Paragraph One

1. Write a sentence that introduces *sub-topic idea one*.

2. From column one on the previous page, write a sentence about each detail in the boxes.

3. Remember to indent.

_____

_____

_____

_____

_____

_____

_____

_____

_____

_____

_____

A Healthy Body *(cont.)*

Step 2. Package the First Draft *(cont.)*

Write Body Paragraph Two

1. Write a sentence that introduces *sub-topic idea two*.

2. From column two on page 235, write a sentence about each detail in the boxes.

3. Remember to indent.

_____

_____

_____

_____

_____

_____

_____

_____

_____

_____

Write Body Paragraph Three

1. Write a sentence that introduces *sub-topic idea three*.

2. From column three on page 235, write a sentence about each detail in the boxes.

3. Remember to indent.

_____

_____

_____

_____

_____

_____

_____

_____

_____

A Healthy Body *(cont.)*

Step 2. Package the First Draft *(cont.)*

Write the Concluding Paragraph

1. Concluding paragraphs can *summarize* what was written in the essay, *come to a conclusion* based on the evidence, or *re-state the introduction*.

2. Concluding paragraphs always show closure, the writer's way of saying goodbye to the reader.

3. Remember to indent.

_____

_____

_____

_____

_____

_____

_____

_____

_____

_____

_____

_____

_____

_____

_____

_____

Step 3. Prune and Plump: Use the Revise and Edit Checklist (page 17) to guide revisions to the first draft. Make revisions by erasing or using a different-colored pen to over-write on the first draft.

Step 4. Polish and Re-Write: Use the Revise and Edit Checklist (page 17) to guide editing. Erase and re-write or use different-colored pen to over-write. After final editing, write an attractive copy or use word processing.

Step 5. Publish and Perform: Store in a portfolio, read aloud, post on the wall.

Caring Comments

Adam

Adam is tall.

Adam is nice.

He is smart.

I like Adam.

Adam is tall and athletic, he plays ball well.

Adam is a good student.

Adam never criticizes others.

Adam is friendly.

Adam's family invites me to go with them.

Adam is the smartest boy I know.

Adam's eyes are bright.

Adam is generous.

Melissa

Melissa is smart.

Melissa is very thoughtful and kind.

I like Melissa. Sometimes, when she is sick, she is grouchy,
but it is not really her, it is her illness and she bounces right back.

Melissa is so cool, all the boys like her.

Melissa is very smart. She never makes a bad grade.

Melissa is totally awesome, and all that.

Melissa is my new friend; I hope she never moves away,

but I know she will move away very soon to a farm.

Melissa can play ball like a boy.

Melissa is a good friend.

I like Melissa because she stands up for herself and others.

Caring Comments *(cont.)*

Name_____   Date_____

From time to time, it is good to assess your fellow sojourners in a positive, nurturing, and gentle way. As you prepare to leave one era of your life and begin another, take this time to reflect upon what each person in your group has meant to you. Remember, positive comments only.

(   ) _____

_____

_____

(   ) _____

_____

_____

(   ) _____

_____

_____

(   ) _____

_____

_____

(   ) _____

_____

_____

(   ) _____

_____

_____

(   ) _____

_____

_____

(   ) _____

_____

_____